THE OLD PLANTATION:

How We Lived in the Great House and Cabin Before The War,

Annotated and Illustrated.

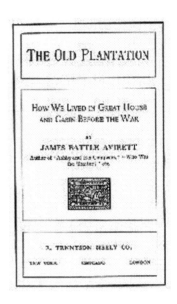

THE OLD PLANTATION: How We Lived in the Great House and Cabin Before the War, Annotated and Illustrated.

By James Battle Avirett, D. D. (1901)

Annotation and illustration research by Lucy Booker Roper (2015)

Because of the addition of annotations, biographical sketches, explanations of archaic terms and regional dialect for the modern reader, translations of foreign phrases often seen in 19th century writing, as well as added illustrations, this particular edition, re-typeset and formatted; constitutes a new intellectual property, and is therefore © 2014 by Lucy Booker Roper.

CONTENTS

ABOUT THE AUTHOR

THIS picture of Dr. Avirett and his camp-servant "Black Hawk", (John A. Jackson) was taken after the war when Dr. Avirett spoke at the dedication of the monument to the New Market cadets in Lexington, Virginia, 1903.

James Battle Avirett was an Episcopalian priest, writer, and Confederate chaplain from North Carolina. Born on the Averitt plantation (near New River Chapel and the present town of Richlands), Avirett, who took on this particular spelling of his family name, was a scholar at the University of North Carolina from 1850 through 1852. In 1861 he was ordained to the Episcopal diaconate, and subsequently became a chaplain to the

Seventh Virginia Cavalry (known as Ashby's Cavalry). Upon Avirett's death, he was said to have been the longest living Confederate chaplain.

Following is his obituary from the Confederate Veteran magazine, Volume 20, January 1912:

Rev. James Battle Avirett, D. D., died at the Western Maryland Hospital, where he had gone for medical treatment. Dr. Avirett, until almost up to the time of his death, apparently enjoyed fairly good health. On his last day in this life he chatted with a friend in the sun parlor, and had just repaired to his room and lain down upon his couch when he died.

Dr. Avirett was the fifth son of John Alfred Avirett, a French Huguenot, and Susan (Thomas) Averitt. He was one of nine children, and was born March 12, 1835. His birth took place near New Berne, North Carolina. He graduated at Chapel Hill University with the late Senator Vance. He practiced law at Mobile and Selma, Alabama, and Raleigh, North Carolina, until 1858, when he took up his studies for the ministry. In 1861, he was ordained by Bishop Meade at Staunton, Virginia, and became chaplain of the 7th Virginia Cavalry at Winchester under Ashby, and was the first chaplain to receive a commission as such in the Confederate army. In 1862 Dr. Avirett married Mary, daughter of Philip Williams.

At the close of the war, he established at Winchester the Dunbar Female Institute, which became widely known in that section. Later he returned to the ministry and went to Maryland in 1870 as a missionary under Bishop William Pinkney. From there he took charge of Silver Spring and Rockville, In Montgomery County, Maryland, remaining the rector in charge for sixteen years, during which time, he added three chapels to the parish. He next took charge at Upper Marlborough, Prince George County, and from there moved to Waterville, New York. Next he was at

Oswego, N. Y., and in 1904 went from there to Kittrell, near Raleigh, North Carolina.

Because of failing health, he located among old friends at Buena Vista, near Lexington, Virginia. In the fall of 1908 his wife died. After that he made his home with his son, Col. John W. Avirett, at Rose Hill.

Aside from his ministerial attainments, Dr. Avirett was a versatile writer, and contributed many articles to magazines and Church papers. He was also the author of the following books: "Ashby and his Compeers," "The Old Plantation, "The South before the War," and "The Real Jackson." These books attest the scholarly attainments of their author.

A Southerner of the true type, Dr. Avirett was loyal to the cause for which he fought. It was permitted this old soldier of the Confederacy to see a reunited country and to lay the olive branch of peace upon the graves of some who wore the blue as well as those who wore the gray. After making his home in Cumberland, Dr. Avirett assisted in the services of the Emmanuel Episcopal Church.

He is buried at Mount Hebron Cemetery, Winchester, Virginia.

Review in a magazine from 1900:

"Rev. James Battle Avirett was raised in Orange County, his father being one of the wealthiest in that region. He has in this work faithfully and interestingly shown the light and shadows of life on a large plantation, stocked with slaves, under the wise control of a high minded, conscientious overseer. It is an excellent antidote to the poison fastened in the mind by Mrs. Stowe's pen portrait of Legare and his iniquities. The exciting stories of 'coon hunts, and the humorous incidents, which diversify the more grave sketches of slave character, make the book a favorite with the youngest readers." ("North Carolina University Magazine," vol. xviii, November 1900, page 257.)

Acknowledged as the foremost biographer of Turner Ashby, Rev. James B. Avirett (1835-1912) was on the move with the 7th Virginia Cavalry brandishing the sword of the Spirit and the sword of corporeal defender of the Valley of Virginia.

INTRODUCTION.

ACTION and reaction — ebb and flow — seem to be the rule of life in its varied manifestations. Winter and Summer — Seedtime and Harvest, with their death into life — are in striking illustration of this rule. To the benumbing influences of that form of imperialism which swept over Europe, holding down as in a vise all effort at asserted individuality in citizenship, the student of history and its philosophies will recollect, came slow but sure reaction. Coming in form of the French Revolution, it was far, very far, from being an unmixed blessing. It liberated the individual from everybody and everything but himself. This it was powerless to do, because in its chaos it refused to recognize the condition precedent of all healthful life. It turned a deaf ear to the great truth, in its blind worship of Reason, that Order is Heaven's first Law. A power so strong as this social cyclone, working in the orbit of human weakness, could not be confined to France. It overleaped the channel and, though strongly resisted by the conservative forces of Anglo-Saxon England, it has left its influence upon that virile polity which had successfully withstood the mutations of centuries. Entrenching itself in Exeter Hall, London, it threw its forces across the Atlantic and fortified them in Faneuil Hall, Boston.

And thus it came about that it was the benumbing shadows of the French Revolution, in its contempt for law, order and precedent, which left such giants in the state as Mr. Webster, and Bishop Hopkins of Vermont in the Church without a counteracting following. Thus it was that the John Brown Raid, called into being by that bold, bad, strong book, "Uncle Tom's Cabin," proved to be the *avant-coureur* (harbinger) of the Civil War.

The South, possessing her soul in patience, has waited. Yes! wretchedly misunderstood, we have waited for the pendulum of public opinion to swing around to our side of the arc. God only knows in what bitterness of heart we have waited. We have waited in full loyalty to the Government, both State and Federal, and though in waiting we may not have grown strong, yet we have waited long enough, under the inspiring example and memory of the Christian Lee at Lexington, Virginia, to be full of hope that the tide is now setting in from the high seas of error, and that the day of our vindication in the world's judgment is nigh at hand.

Faneuil Hall, Boston. Peter Faneuil (1700 –1743) was a wealthy American colonial merchant, slave trader, and humanitarian who donated Faneuil Hall to Boston.

Men, very thoughtful men, lacking in no element of manly loyalty to the powers that be, are free to assert that in the reaction which has set in, erroneous views as to the causes which led up to the war, as well as the facts in its conduct, are giving place to the truth. The Supreme Court of the country, in its appellate jurisdiction of last resort is affirming and reaffirming the constitutional doctrine of Statehood in its distinct autonomy. Public opinion from the lakes to the gulf, is voicing American utterance as to the superiority of the Caucasian race. From ocean to ocean there is a growing recognition that the tide has turned, in the steadily increasing thrift of the South. And thus it would seem to be that all things come to him who waits.

The writer of this book, the chaplain on the staff of that matchless Cavalier, Gen. Turner Ashby, Chief of Cavalry under Stonewall Jackson, has patiently waited for nearly forty years to tell his own story. While envy, hatred and malice ruled the hour, he well knew that it would be worse than "Love's Labor Lost," to do anything but wait—bide his time. He has waited until he hears falling from the lips of the distinguished Senator Hoar of Massachusetts largely the same arguments in his opposition to the imperialism at Manila as were employed by Southern .senators in the United States Senate in the spring of 1861. He has waited until Colonel Henderson of the British Army, in his "Life of Stonewall Jackson," has placed Lee's lieutenant in the forefront of the world's great captains; and in doing so he has shown in a very striking manner that the appeal, which the silence of the South has slowly brought about, is largely vindicatory of her men and measures. He has waited, until the social conditions at the South before the war are necessarily assuming the misty forms of traditions, and will presently, unless rescued, become to the oncoming generations of the South as mythical as much of the Roman and Grecian stories. He has waited until to wait longer would be treasonable to duty. Having waited long, he now writes in loyalty to past generations of the South—such men and women as those from whom sprang such pure patriots as Robert E. Lee and Stonewall Jackson, and that incomparable army of Northern Virginia and their comrades in gray all over the Southland.

In vindicating his people from the ignorant aspersions of "Uncle Tom's Cabin" and kindred exhalations from a distempered brain, he indulges in no criminations or recriminations. To the ex parte statement of this gifted member of a very gifted family, he simply says what the good old Common Law has said in all its wise judgments, *"Audi alteram partem"*[1] — the wisdom of which legal maxim is further promulged by that higher injunction, "Judge nothing before the time."

The author, a University man and bred to the law, has given nearly forty years of his life under the auspices of the Episcopal Church. We would, therefore, expect a thoughtful book from him. Born and reared to full manhood on one of the largest plantations on tidewater, North Carolina, one will see that with him is the great advantage of writing as an eyewitness, and not from hearsay or second hand. Urged to write this book by such men of the South as the late United States Senator Vance of North Carolina, and encouraged therein by the Bishop of Central New York and others of his Northern friends, we think he has justified their appreciation of his capacity for this work.

---

[1] *Audi alteram partem* means, "hear the other side too", or "hear the alternative party too."

Turner Ashby (1828-1862)

The reader will observe that he takes hold of none of the many weak threads in the sensational and overwrought story, "Uncle Tom's Cabin," which he might well have done by showing that the worst character in the book is a New Englander, while the best is largely the product of those social forces which Mrs. Stowe is undermining. He simply tells you how the servants on his father's estate were treated, and unfolds, under that treatment, the gradual uplift of a pagan race to that point of high character, which, in the judgment (?) of those in power, fitted them for all the high duties of that citizenship so gracefully adorning such men as Chauncey Depew and Mark Hanna.

In laying the scene of his recitals on his father's plantation he is fortunate in knowing whereof he speaks, and he does not intimate that the treatment of the servants there was in anywise more humane than elsewhere in the South. In his painstaking portrayal of the social conditions on this plantation, of which he could write both creditably and intelligently, he says: "*Ex uno disce omnia.*"[2] Of all the arguments in his contention with Mrs. Stowe, our author uses this one most tellingly. He says if the system of labor on Southern estates was so cruel and barbarous, if the Negroes were slaves abject and not servants trusted and well cared for, why was it that when the Southern homes were stripped of their defenders, then in the Confederate armies, the Negroes did not reenact the bloody scenes of San Domingo—why did they not rise, with blazing torch in hand, and kill and burn? By so doing, in eight and forty hours they could have broken up the organized Confederate armies in front of Richmond and Atlanta, whose soldiers would have rushed back home to protect their wives and children. And yet, not one single torch of incendiarism was kindled. If any change came, the Negroes of the old plantation, conscious of their power, were more loyal and tenderly dutiful than at any time in their history.

No! No! The truth is, as shown on these pages, the institution had knit the hearts of the two races together too tenderly, in the happy life on the old plantation, to suggest to either race any such bloody event. The Negro of the South to-day knows, that when in trouble his best friend is his old master or his children; and if left alone by those who understand neither race at the South, he would reflect this knowledge in all the relations of life and the race problem of the South would be solved—not in the penalties of odious lynch law, but in the displacement of the fiendish crimes which lead up to it.

---

[2] "From one thing you can discern all."

THE OLD PLANTATION.

CHAPTER I.

A look at the different cultures of the "Puritan" and the "Cavalier."

"Let fate do her worst, there are relics of joy,
  Bright dreams of the past which she cannot destroy,
  Which come in the night time of sorrow and care
  And bring back the features which love used to wear.
  Long, long be my heart with such memories filled,
  Like the vase in which roses have once been distilled—
You may break, you may shatter the vase, if you will,
  But the scent of the roses will hang round it still."

TO the carefully discriminating mind nothing can be clearer than the following proposition: At Gettysburg, at Chickamauga and elsewhere, every memorial stone, cemented with gratitude for patriotic devotion to country, which has been erected either by Government or individuals, is in strong attestation of the social forces and political conditions which made the armies of the United States such terrible realities.

At the South in Richmond, Virginia, in Winchester, in Raleigh, North Carolina, in fact all over the broad area embraced by the Confederacy, every effort made to perpetuate the memories of the wearers of the gray—every grassy hillock in God's acre or elsewhere marking the last bivouac of the men who followed Lee, Jackson and others —proclaims in trumpet tones the strength of the silent, subtle forces which underlay the grand struggle for Southern independence, expressed in separate and distinct autonomy.

It is both fitting and just that these stones should have been so raised on both sides. The carping criticism which would deny to either the precious privilege of honoring its dead is foreign to the patriotic devotion which called into existence those martial hosts which shook the continent in 1861 and '65. It is eminently natural and proper that both sections, which were lately arrayed in such bitter hostility, should accord to and join with each other in those high and holy observances, which perpetuate the fame of those men, now rapidly becoming the property of a common country. The time is nigh at hand when all over this broad land the proud distinction of American citizen, so nobly worn by Robert E. Lee, Stonewall Jackson, Forrest, Hampton, et id omne genus, (transl. "and everything of the sort") will cause a thrill of high admiration, as well among the dwellers along our northern lakes as in the breasts of those who live amid the savannahs of the South. And this is so rightly, because naturally. It is well-nigh axiomatic that a people which does not cherish with loving heart the memory of ancestral virtues will enrich its posterity with scant legacy. If then it be true that the memory of our dead is a duty, God imposed and heaven blessed, is it not both wise and profitable to analyze these social forces, which entered so largely into the formation of the character of those noble men, as well in the Army of the Potomac, led by Grant at the close of the struggle, as those who confronted them in battle's stern array for four long years, led by Lee? To the casual, careless observer there was a general sameness in high valor and devotion to duty, as seen in Hancock and Jackson and their followers. To the painstaking, patient student of history and its philosophies differentiations appear, as deep and broad as those, which the careful study of Wellington and Napoleon brings to light. If it is true that the child is the father of the man—that we are all of us marvelously molded by the nursery influences at the mother's knee—that men out in the struggle with the world, in after years, are largely the product of hearthstone forces in childhood, then must we seek for some cause at home, in the structure of society,

14

some one or more institutional forces, characterizing the environment and accounting for the difference between the people of the North and South.

It will not satisfy the alert mind to say that these differences in products, customs, habits, propelling powers in every-day life—those subtle differences in the mainspring of action—are traceable to differences in the climate. There is much in this. In the economy of nature the sun, with heat and light differing in varying degrees of latitude and longitude, stamps these differences on the orange groves of Florida, full of bloom and beauty, as well as upon the bleak, cold fisheries on the coast of Maine. In the natural world climate is self-asserting and supreme. In the higher forms of life, when one passes into the realms of those strong forces swayed by the supernatural, where mind and spirit, acting either separately or conjointly, leave their enduring impress, do we not meet with products which deny and defy the strong influences of climate? It is true that climate has much, but not all to do in making us what we are. Soil and climate influence and determine avocations or pursuits in life in no small degree. The many and marked points of difference between an agricultural and manufacturing or commercial community determine largely the habits of life, modes of thought and in some sense, the standards of action characterizing the two people of the North and South.

At one time, in old England and elsewhere in Europe, under the unifying forces of one and the same environment, we were solidly one and the same people. When the exodus from Europe began social differences had already asserted themselves and to such a degree that in many respects the earlier settlers of New England differed largely from those who settled Maryland, Virginia and the Carolinas. It is very difficult to satisfactorily account for these differences. Climate could have had but little to do with those differences which so strikingly obtained between those men who trod the decks of the Mayflower and those who followed Sir Walter Raleigh, that matchless Cavalier, of whom

15

our own Lowell, in his inscription for the Raleigh memorial window in St. Margaret's Church, England, has so beautifully said:

"The new world's sons, from England's breast we drew
Such milk, as bids remember whence we came;
Proud of her past where from our future grew,
This window we inscribe with Raleigh's fame."

The Gallic civilization, repressing and depressing, until at last Spain, in the loss of her American colonies, has nigh disappeared from among the nations of the earth, tells its own story of the influence of government upon the governed. If it be true, that the character of the government asserts itself in the character of its subjects— if, in other words, bad laws make a bad people—we think it equally susceptible of demonstration that whether the word of God occurs in the constitutional charter of its life and liberty or not a people's religion always expresses itself in the character of their government.

So strikingly true is this that the gifted John S. Pendleton[3] of Virginia was once heard to say that he never left his home in Piedmont, Virginia, and went as United States Minister to Brazil that, after a residence of six months in Rio de Janeiro, he was not forced to realize that he was a worse man than when he left his home in the United States.

So much for the influence of environment and the subtle effects of government and religion on the temper and disposition of a man. When crystallized, these constitute his character. It will

_____

[3] John Strother Pendleton (1802 –1868), called "The Lone Star", was a nineteenth-century member of the Virginia House of Delegates, U.S. congressman — elected both in 1845 and 1847, diplomat, lawyer and farmer from Virginia. Pendleton earned his nickname, "The Lone Star" because he was the only Whig member from Virginia.

appear from this line of thought that when in the early settlement of this country, in the two sets of colonies of New England and Virginia, marked differences were at once recognized— the Puritan and the Cavalier on social lines were far apart. In the former of these two orders of civilization, the Puritan, there were many and marked excellences. The world has rarely, if ever seen among any people a higher standard of general thrift, the outcome largely of their industry and frugality. The marked influence they have exerted on the policy of this country, because of the large wealth they have amassed, is a striking comment on their methods and measures from a material standpoint. Their untiring energy; their calm self-containedequilibrium; their ability at all times and under all circumstances to give themselves the full benefit of their resourcefulness; in the main, the absence of both breadth of acres and fertility of their landed estates; the marked intellectuality of many of their public men, anterior to and during the revolution; the deep set influence of the leading dogma of their religious faith as held by the masterful Jonathan Edwards—these and other causes, under the influence of climate, made the New England civilization a wonderful lever in the up-building of the young republic. And yet there were some aspects in which this civilization was very weak. It is in a large measure that weakness which is always found in those conditions caused by a dense population, with its numerous large towns and cities, the outcome of manufacturing and commercial enterprises wrought out by energy into a marked success. There is more truth than this materialistic age is willing to allow in the trite old saying, "That man made the town and God made the country." The various forms of social distemper, with which the human race in all ages have been accursed, have had their origin in those congested conditions of life found in thickly settled communities. The old writer was not far away from the truth when he said that cities were ulcers and the smaller towns were boils on the body politic. Men in closely aggregated relations will do and dare

17

(mostly evil things) what they would scarcely think of in segregated homes. The happiest, proudest days of the republic came to us in those healthier conditions of smaller cities, with a scattered population, when the pure air and healthful sunshine of the country life were strong in the coinage, if not in the Spartan simplicity, of those influences; when the criminal dockets of our courts were far shorter and we had no penitentiaries.

The Cavalier civilization, with its centers in the South, was, in many particulars, different from the Puritan. A close study of history will discover the fact that it brought across the ocean less of that restlessness and more of that restfulness, which naturally inhere in those conditions of respect for authority and precedents than was found among our Northern brethren. The continuity of these conditions accounts for the absence, in all her fair borders, of those "isms" which, like wasteful and destructive parasites, sap the very life out of a people's faith, both in God and in each other.

One may be on the point of enquiring what was it that constituted the people of the old South so especially a peculiar people, and, if not strikingly zealous of good works, yet enabled them to exert a strong influence in their day and generation? The ready answer is close at hand. The Southern people, prior to 1865, were a plantation people and were patriarchal, in a sense and to a degree unknown in any part of this country before or since. What : enabled them to lead this order of life? Largely of one blood, living on large estates in the employment of their African servants, there was among them, in the absence of manufacturing and large commercial centers, that freedom from restless change, which can alone be hoped for in any community in the perfect absence of those sharp antagonisms between Capital and Labor. At the South these two mighty giants, whose wrestlings have aforetime vexed governments and overturned empires, were at peace. And this was so because, to put it epigrammatically, our Capital was our Labor and our Labor was our Capital. Hence it was, in the old South, we were enabled to present that enviable condition of fixedness and stability which came with families for generations living with their servants on the same ancestral estates. With us our household gods were not often removed and, in consequence, there attached to our lares and penates (ancestral homes) that peculiar sanctity and reverence, which gave rise to that blessed form of friendliness, which will be long, long remembered, as the old-fashioned, openhearted Southern hospitality.

The object of this volume, now in hand, is to describe one of these old plantations—its occupants, white and colored—the exact relations between the two races; the conditions under which they served each other; the character of the houses in which they both dwelt; what manner of food they ate; their daily duties and amusements; their religion; in fine, to draw from memory a picture as an eye witness, as a participant in and a creature of those social forces which made the old South a power in the land. Gladly would I draw such a truthful, detailed and minute picture, as will teach the young people of this and upcoming generations, both in the North and South, what manner of men and women lived south of the Susquehanna river prior to the late war between the States.

This, to the writer, in his old age, will be a labor of love. Here and there he may seem to dwell on some feature of his recital with great minuteness. If so, it is because in no portion of the world has there ever been, or will there ever be again, such happy social conditions as formerly existed in the old South on the old plantation.

Were it not that the present writer has peculiar advantages in treating his subject—himself in every fiber of his organism, mental, moral and physical, the creation, the outcome of the plantation life—he might draw back and remain silent in the presence of the deep prejudice and painful ignorance still in existence against the institutional life of his people. However, he must write. He must tell his own story and put forth a friendly, if

19

it be a weak hand, to rescue from oblivion the story of the old plantation life. It is now to many people very nebulous, and will soon become so very misty as to be mythical. He is prompted to write in vindication of his own people, in the knowledge of the fact that on a large plantation, with hundreds of servants, his father and mother were the only two slaves upon it. Years ago the writer's old friend, the distinguished late Senator Z. B. Vance, that wonderful tribune of the people, urged him to do what he is now attempting—saying that only the product of plantation life could tell the story authentically, as an eye witness, and not writing from hearsay or second hand.

Recently the writer has received letters from President Alderman, and ex-President Battle of the University of North Carolina, as well as from such distinguished citizens of the South as Dr. Hunter McGuire of Virginia; Messrs. Graham Daves, James A. Bryan, Oscar W. Blacknall, Generals William H. Cheek, and Julian S. Carr; Rev. Doctors Hufham and Yates of North Carolina—all urging him to carry his book on to completion. Obliged, after a ministry of nearly forty years, to take some rest, in consequence of failing health, the writer hopes he has elected wisely to rest by changing his labor. He wishes most heartily that he were younger and could bring to the discharge of these high duties the verve and élan, the vigor of more meridian powers; but, if much younger, he would) have missed the boon of a plantation education under the purer and happier days of the Republic, when citizenship at the South was happily exempt from those saddening forms of change and decay which, in these latter days, have come from bad politics and worse statesmanship growing out of a cheapened and debauched ballot. It saddens one to attempt to realize how depressed our own Washington, Hamilton, Jay, Jefferson and Madison would become could they come back to the once familiar scenes, which they glorified by their high type of patriotic devotion, and witness for themselves the painful decadence of citizenship, as well at the North by reason of foreignism as at the South because of the Ethiopian ballot.

And yet we must not despair of the Republic. In no country, in the world's history, have the vital forces been quite so strong as in these United States. There is a virgin freshness, combined with a masculine strength, in this young land of ours which will not tolerate the baneful forms of pessimism, and which, if not inspiring, at least suggests that he is the true friend of the country whose form of optimism urges one to work on, to hope on, for the best. We are far too young as a people to have so far crystallized in habits and views (which if wrong) as to be beyond the reach of remedy. We older Southern people are proud of and thankful for the blessed days of the old South. We will endeavor to teach our offspring to cherish the memories and emulate the virtues of the antebellum civilization. Full well we know that no portion of human history has been more ignorantly misunderstood or painfully misjudged than the slaveholding era of the South. It has been more bitter than defeat itself to realize with sickening certainty the fact that until recently we have been denied the privilege of setting the world right in the matter of the causes which led up to, as well as the conduct of the struggle, whose epitaph the major part of Christendom would write in the words: "Lost Cause." Second, sober thought, governmental experiment in heretofore untried suffrage problems—the cold hard facts of nearly four decades in our history—are bringing on marked changes in the opinion of very many thoughtful people. Some of the very best thinkers, men enlightened by the culture of the philosophies of history, are already declaring that it was only in the matter of physical force and results that General Lee surrendered to General Grant.

"If lost, 'twas false;
If true, it was not lost."

The Supreme Court of the United States, by recent decisions, is maintaining the doctrine of States' Rights with separate autonomy. The signs of the times are hopeful, when, though sad the necessity, Senator Hoar of Massachusetts, in antagonizing imperialism at Manila and elsewhere, is using largely the same arguments which Mr. Jefferson Davis employed in justifying the action of the South in 1860 and '61, in the Senate of the United States, just prior to the secession of the Southern States.

CHAPTER II.

Points out that George Washington, Jefferson, Madison, Monroe, Henry, and such others as gave dignity and honor to American citizenship were slave-holders.

WHEN one crosses out of the little State of Delaware into the historic commonwealth of Maryland, looking to the south and west, there stretches away before him a magnificent domain. Temperate in climate, diversified in soil, richly embellished with hill and dale, in many respects it is unequaled by any in the world. It is traversed by the Alleghany and Blue Ridge mountains, with foothills which gradually lose themselves in the sea coast counties, and is watered by such beautiful rivers as will come to mind when you think of the Potomac, the James, the Roanoke, the Savannah, the Alabama, the Rio Grande and the lordly Mississippi. These rivers drain large valleys and water sheds, whose soil in many portions rivals the fertility of the Nile. This section is blessed indeed by a loving Providence in those innumerable medicinal springs, whose waters are given for the healing of earth's diseased children. Surely when one has familiarized himself with the picturesque valley of the Shenandoah, in dear old Virginia; or has allowed his eye to sweep over the blue-grass region of Kentucky; or has drunk in the beauties of that famous cloudland country in the vicinity of Asheville, in western North Carolina—where the laughing waters of the beautiful French Broad (mirroring the forms of the grandest mountains east of the incomparable Rockies), go on their way rejoicing to tell it out to the sunlit Gulf of Mexico— that here, in the old Southland, is the Eldorado of the world. Surely when one has done this he feels like exclaiming, as does the Neapolitan when he looks upon Naples, "Behold this fair land

and then die, for there is nothing more beautiful to be seen on earth."

It does not lie in the province of these short annals to indulge in any elaborate description of this famous section of our country, which has proven such an important factor in the rapid development of our young republic. And yet, common justice demands that something should be said of its wonderful products, notably so of its splendid product of noble men and fair women, which has put the world in love with the very finest type of Anglo-Saxon civilization. Think of her forests, under the shade of whose oaks the Druids might worship, and under whose wide spreading beech trees Virgil's fair Amaryllis might have been wooed and won. Think of her grand old hickories, graceful ashes, and above all those lordly pines, in whose branches the wind is ever sighing out the lullaby of old ocean; her magnificent magnolias, from whose flower-swayed branches, our incomparable mocking-bird, night and day, is pouring out his roundelay of love, in notes sweeter far than these of the Oriental nightingale.

Time fails one in telling fully of the wealth, both of the useful and the beautiful, which a beneficent Creator has given us in these widespread forests of the South. Would you speak of flowers? Nowhere on God's green earth does the rich, blushing rose (that century-sceptered queen of lovely Flora) reach higher perfection than in the flower gardens of Raleigh, North Carolina, or in those of Pensacola, Florida. All of our Southern flowers, which represent those exact adjustments of heat and light involved in the higher ranges of color and perfume, find here their fullest requirements. Would you speak of fruits? Think of the luscious Georgia peach, the vermeil on whose cheek equals that of the lovely damsels who pluck and eat them; the melons, the apples, the pears, the nectarines, the figs, the apricots and the luscious grapes, equal to Eschol's clusters, and her oranges as well— in fine, of all her fruits; and while your mouth waters say that nature in dear old Southland has done her best. Would you like nuts with your coffee after dinner? We have walnuts of both varieties, the pecan, the hickory nut, and the more delicate scaly or shell bark, the famous peanut, and even the delicate, dainty, little grass nut of the well-appointed Southern garden.

Would you know how it comes about that the cuisine of Baltimore and New Orleans is the wonder and delight of the world? Associate in your mind the fact that "all flesh is grass" with a fine sirloin of blue-grass beef in the South and the noble saddles of Southdown mutton (fatted on this same grass and flavored by browsing the sheep on the budding twigs in our mountain lots), and you will cease to wonder why both New Yorkers and Philadelphians go to the White Sulphur and Capon Springs of Virginia, not only to rest, but to laugh and grow fat as well.

Would you tell me that the perfection of fish is found in the markets of Southern Europe, or to be had at Delmonico's in New York, or in Boston? This is not so. Grant that the wealthy people of the large Northern cities demand that the "pick" of the Chesapeake or Albemarle "catch" shall be carried to them. The power of wealth is very great, but it cannot control nature. The fine shad and other varieties are carried, but in the carriage they lose their finest flavor, and thus the millionaire feeds, in some sense, upon stale fish. When you have eaten the planked shad in full view of the lovely Chesapeake Bay, or have been so fortunate as to enjoy the pompano fish,* that perfection of the Gulf waters, at the old Saint Charles in New Orleans, you will understand how kindly in her dispensations dear old dame nature has been, and still is, to her sunburnt, unconventional Southern children, far away from Gotham and "the hub of civilization," so called. Before passing away from the Southern products, let us not forget her canvasback duck nor her diamondback terrapin. We will not discount that miracle of delicate flavor and toothsomeness, the oysters of our Southern waters, the perfection of which is claimed in the "Broad Creekers" and the "New River catch" of the North Carolina market. At the South, notably so in those blessed

25

days before the flood of 1861 and 1865, our very finest product was the old-fashioned ham of the Southern plantation. More time would be required than can be given it in the description of those conditions which lead up to this time-honored, ancestral essential to a good dinner in its full excellence. In the old South no dinner was in any sense complete without that lordly dish, which always confronted the mistress of the plantation at the head of the table, after the soup and fish had been discussed. Later on we will take a slice out of that old ham. Just now we must go on.

The old South was essentially a people of plantations, as distinguished from farms. Of cities there were but few, and these not strikingly large. Baltimore, New Orleans, St. Louis and Charleston were among the largest; and while there were other smaller cities and towns—in wealth, in political power, in social influence, the most attractive feature of our life—the strength and the charm were in the country. This was so because the South was strikingly an agricultural people. From the greater fixedness and certainty of their possessions, in broad acreage and numerous servants, few of her people had been stung by the gadfly of millionarism, more poisonous than the asp, which sucked the blood from Cleopatra's purple veins. They were content to enjoy the profits from producing their various staples of cotton, rice, sugar, tobacco, naval stores and lumber; they were content to live and let live; in doing but very little to build up their commerce or manufactories, but allowing others to transform their products for the markets of the world and thus grow rich.

Pending this long period of unwritten agreement between the North and the South, the former producing largely and the latter manufacturing the products of the United States, all Europe stood in wonder at the rapid development in both sections. The perfect comity between the two demonstrated to the world, in far more forceful form than dear old Aesop embodied it in his striking fable of the bundle of sticks, that "in union is strength."

Saddening indeed is the fact that during a period of national dementia sullen sectionalism sapped the Union of strength to such a degree as to almost make the once fair young republic the laughing-stock of the world. Fortunately reaction supervened in the return of that brotherhood, which indeed is the procuring cause of our present colossal proportions.

Having already glanced at the extent of territory embraced in the old South, with her varied agricultural products, her untold riches in climate and soil, her vast resources in forest wealth and inexhaustible mines of coal and iron, together with those rich contributions both of comfort and wealth which her waters gave as they teemed with life, there is something still which must be said of the richest of all her gifts to national wealth—her population—the men and women who dwelt upon their ancestral estates.

The time is past for any defense of African slavery— an institution which some say cannot be defended. But it must be allowed that its practical working at the old South among our ancestors was such, in the language of Mr. Henry Grady, "as to challenge and hold our loving respect." In no time in the history of our race has there ever been seen a peasantry so happy, and in every respect so well to do, as the Negro slaves of America. We are to indulge in no criminations or recriminations as to who introduced them into this country. We are not now to inquire who they were who held so tenaciously to the carrying trade of these poor pagans and (in many cases) cannibals from the coast of Africa, through the ports, first of the colonies and then of the United States, into the landed estates of this country, North and South. We are not now to tell it out to the world, that family secret of ours, as to what was the basis of some of the largest fortunes still in existence among us. We shall be silent as to what portion of this country was represented in Congress by those favoring the extension or the abolition of the slave trade. We do not propose to allow our family soiled linen to be washed in the front yard of the world's unfriendly criticism. This would argue the absence of good taste and gentle breeding and might provoke an unpleasant state of affairs. But, guarded as we may be in keeping our family secrets, it is both curious and profitable, if sometimes humiliating, to note how murder will out. Lynx-eyed history is both persistent and insistent in gathering up and getting facts. Among the ancients Cupid was represented as blind, while Justice always wore a bandage over her fair eyes. In this electric age history courageously and successfully insists upon having her telescope for long ranged views of the truth, while she will not be denied her microscope for more minute investigations.

We are quite willing to leave the position, which our forefathers at the South occupied, on this social question to the solemn, God-fearing utterances of history. We would simply say that the civilized world stood amazed at the social conditions at the South during the eventful years of 1861 and '65. These slaves (so called)—these servants —during that time with loving fidelity guarded the homes of their masters, absent in many cases with those armies that barred their way to freedom. This condition of affairs has been so happily (because forcibly, truthfully) presented by a distinguished son of Georgia, Mr. Grady, that extracts are here made from his brilliant, brave hearted paper.

"If 'Uncle Tom's Cabin' had portrayed the rule of slavery at the South rather than the rarest exception, not all the armies that went to the field could have stayed the flood of rapine and arson and pillage that would have started with the first gun of the Civil War. Instead of that, witness the miracle of the slave, in loyalty to his master, closing the fetters upon his own limbs—maintaining and defending the families of those who fought against his freedom—and at night, on the far-off battlefield, searching among the carnage for his young master, that he might lift the dying head to his breast and bend to catch the last word to the old folks at home; so wrestling in the meantime in agony and love that he would lay down his life in his master's stead. History has no parallel to the faith kept by the Negro in the South during

28

the war. Often five hundred Negroes to a single white man, and yet through these dusky throngs the women and children walked in safety and the unprotected home rested in peace. Unmarshaled, the black battalion moved patiently to the fields in the morning to feed the armies their idleness would have starved and at night gathered anxiously at the great house to hear the news from master, though conscious that his victory made their chains enduring. Everywhere humble and kindly. Everywhere the bodyguard of the helpless. Everywhere the rough companion of the little ones. The silent sentry in his lowly cabin. The shrewd counsellor. And when the dead came home, a mourner at the open grave. A thousand torches would have disbanded every Southern army, but not one was lighted. When the master, going to the war in which slavery was involved, said to his slave, 'I leave my home and loved ones in your charge,' the tenderness between the man and master stood disclosed. Its patriarchal features were revealed."

The Southern people are daily thanking this golden mouthed son of Georgia for this and many other matchless utterances in Boston and New York, as well as for his daily teaching at home, in which he taught each section by no false position, but by simply presenting the truth in naked majesty, to love each other back into lasting peace. Would God had spared him a few more years in his bright and beautiful life, to have beheld with his own eyes the fine fruitage of his well-nigh divine teachings, inspired by the matchless example and vicarious suffering of Lee at Lexington, Virginia, whom his father loved and followed in the Southern army confronting Grant.

Mr. Grady is right.[4] It is simply impossible for any Northern man, with his hired servants, to comprehend the facts of the

---

[4] Henry Grady (1850- 1889) was a journalist and author from Athens, Georgia. He held positions with the Rome Courier, the Atlanta

patriarchal relation between master and servant, with its friendliness and sympathy of the old plantation life.

Herald, and the New York Herald. He was a brilliant orator and worked for reconciliation of the North and South.

If one spoke the truth of the regime, in painting the picture of the servants on these estates, trusted because open hearted, sympathetic and full of innocent gossip and comradeship, he was once accounted either as a dreamer or as one who drew on his fancy for his facts. But, thank God, this day is passing away. As well under the shadow of Exeter Hall, London, as that of Faneuil Hall, Boston, on both sides of the Atlantic, the representatives of the Anglo-Saxon civilization are reaching out for the truth in a way and to a degree that happily characterizes the closing years of the nineteenth century.

We wish to speak of those social forces which were so actively at work in the South before the war. There must have been some immense force in them to work out such remarkable results, although beleaguered within their own area by the suspicion and the hostility of the outside world. What are the facts? Numerically inferior to the North for the first sixty-four years of the republic, the South furnished the President for fifty-two years. When Great Britain undertook to drive us from the high seas, before our beard had grown, the South, in the United States Senate, forced the war of 1812, with only five Northern senators aiding her. Who commanded our armies at the battle of New Orleans? General Andrew Jackson, a Carolinian. Who were in the lead, when Louisiana, with more than one million square miles of territory, was acquired? Do we not owe the acquisition of Florida to the same source? Who opposed the war with Mexico, by which the vast empire of Texas and New Mexico, together with California, were added to our country? Northern statesmen. Who built the first important railway in this country? Public spirited and wealthy men in Carolina. Where was the first college for girls built but in dear old Georgia, which sent the first steamship across the ocean from the beautiful little city of Savannah? In the world of beautiful nature around us who has gone as deep in her secrets among the birds of the air as our own Audubon? Who has given the commerce of the world such rich instruction in the laws of the winds and the tides and currents of old ocean, mapping and charting them, as Virginia's gifted son, Matthew Fontaine Maury? High up on the roll of the world's great surgeons whose names stand higher than those of Sims and McDonald? To whom in the dark valley of the world's great suffering are we so much indebted as to Crawford Long of Georgia? Whence come John Marshall and Roger Taney, to contest with Judge Story of New England the highest honors and the proudest fame on the Supreme Court Bench of the United States, but from their Southern homes? Who emulated, if they did not surpass, Daniel Webster in the United States Senate, with magnetic thrill and irresistible, inexorable logic? Mr. Clay of Kentucky, and Mr. Calhoun and Mr. Hayne of South Carolina.

Read their history in the nation's eyes," swaying senates and prolonging the life of the republic! "These were a part (and only a part) of the rich contributions which the old South gave to the young nation in trust for the world. And while she was active in doing Bo much for the whole country she was amassing a wealth which, per capita, was greater than that of any other portion of the Union, save, perhaps, that of little Rhode Island. In 1861, if the erring sisters had been allowed to go in peace, was not the disturbing question of the hour: Whence is to come national revenue? Had not this very consideration much to do with the policy of coercion?

"Thus," said Mr. Lincoln, "if we allow the Southern States to depart from the Union, where shall we get the money with which to carry on the Government?"

Those of us who have survived our fondest hopes in many directions are warranted in fearing that the goose that laid the golden egg has been killed. Certainly this matter of finance is one of the vexed problems now confronting us; certainly it does appear that the world Ct at least our part of it, is not growing wiser as it grows older, in many departments of most useful information. But to resume. Let it be said that the presentation of the above facts, embodying the rich contributions to national greatness in most vital, essential particulars which were made by the old South, is very gladly presented. In justifying our ancestral pride it emboldens us in acquainting our children with their rich inheritance, and thus serves to keep erect among us high standards of duty to God and country. It disproves and forever disposes of the loose assertion that the Southern civilization, shadowed by and the product of the institution of slavery, was incapable of high achievements and largely inferior to that of our Northern brethren. It further shows that these Caucasians dwelling on the plantations of the old South, in their guardianship over the millions of Negroes on their estates must, in the main, have treated their servants very kindly. How else can you account for the absence of crime during the war and the presence of such fine forms of mutual kindness among the older persons of both races, as we know exists to this day? It can be emphatically declared, and is often exemplified, that we at the South, the old plantation people and their descendants, do love the race that held the plow, which made the corn that fed the cows that gave the milk that we drank in childhood. It is painful to know how difficult it is to induce those foreign to our condition fully to realize this as a fact, but we, and the Negroes themselves, know that it is so; and we, for the present, must be contented. More light is coming in. Booker Washington in Alabama, and others like him, will go on vindicating the truth of what has been so admirably said on this point by such thoughtful, discriminating men of the South as the late ex-Senator Vance of North Carolina and Mr. Henry Grady of Georgia.

Before leaving this subject it must be allowed one to say in regard to the state of society in the South before the war, that the social conditions in the same community have largely changed. It is said of Mr. Webster that in introducing that charming, typical Southerner, the Honorable George E. Badger, United States Senator of North Carolina, to one of his Boston friends, he employed these words:

Hon. Rufus Choate:

33

"Dear Sir—Permit me to introduce to you the Honorable George E. Badger of North Carolina, your equal and my superior. Yours truly, Daniel Webster."

Thus you will see that in this representative Southerner Mr. Webster recognized the rich product of the South. Yes, say what you may of it, there was an engaging race in the chivalry that tempered even quixotism with dignity, in the piety which saved master and slave alike, in the charity that boasted not, in honor held above estate, in the hospitality that neither condescended nor cringed, in frankness and heartiness and wholesome comradeship, in the reverence paid to womanhood and the inviolable respect in which woman was held, the civilization of the old slave regime in the South has not been surpassed and perhaps will not be equaled among men.

Whence came these fine conditions? We of the old South cannot be blamed (for we are not wrong) in saying that, as there was no hurry among us in those days, no need of haste, men took time to be truly conservative and fastened the tap-root of their every-day life deep down into the soil which was pressed by the foot-prints of George Washington, Jefferson, Madison, Monroe, Henry, and such others as gave dignity and honor to American citizenship. These worthies were all slaveholders, as were Scott and Taylor, and a whole host of others whose devotion to the institutional life of this country gives lustre to many pages of American history.

But it must be borne in mind that the limited space of this volume demands that we hurry on and drop this vein of thought for the present. Yes, drop this vein of thought; not, however, in the sense illustrated by this anecdote. The proprietor of the leading hotel in Savannah, Georgia, ordered old Pompey to bring up on his shoulder from the wharf to the hotel a large sea turtle. Pompey was obeying the order, as with bent shoulders he made his way up the street, the turtle kicking out with his four feet in as many directions. A ventriloquist on the opposite side of the street took in the situation and undertook to have some fun at the old darky's expense. In the most sepulchral tone he could possibly command he threw his voice over the street and, as from the poor turtle, asked, "When is you gwine to drap me?" Instantly, as the turtle went down with a tremendous crash upon the hard pavement, jarring him as though he had been struck by the tail of a whale, the old darky called out, "I'se gwine to drap you right now," and away he went at the most rapid rate, with coat tails flying out as danger signals, in superstitious fright and flight. In the childlike simplicity of the old plantation Negro how much there is both amusing and attractive.

CHAPTER III.

General description of one of the very finest estates in the old South —the author's home place.

IN the South the crops were so various that in no season, however disastrous to some, was there ever a marked failure in all. Each one of these staples had its own peculiar belt or habitat, requiring different modes of culture and special adaptation of soil and climate for its highest perfection. Thus, in the fine wheat lands of Maryland, Virginia and Kentucky, one never saw a field of cotton or sugar cane. Yet all of these crops were the products of the same labor, and while there were peculiar features in the plantation life of the Gulf States' planters, yet there was such a general sameness that in minute description of an estate in North Carolina one furnishes a satisfactory account of them all. In the older States of the South, notably so in Virginia and the Carolinas, there was a more pronounced form of the patriarchal features of the system than was found in the younger States, where the commercial features of the institution more largely obtained. It was not an unusual condition of affairs in the older States that the servants employed came down with broad acreage from father to son for generations. These older States were more influential in giving character to the younger communities of the old South. It was notably so in 1837 and afterwards, because the tide of emigration set out from the Potomac and James Rivers' Valley about that time. We shall select a plantation in North Carolina, the description of which will best illustrate the most healthful forms of the relation of master and servant.

Wherever the uplift of education has been felt there is some one spot where the well-nigh magical influence of home has asserted its power. Some one spot there is to us all where the sky is a little bluer, where the grass is a little greener, where the light of the stars is a little softer, where the song of the birds is sweeter and the south-west breezes of the early spring are much softer; while the perfume of the flowers is far sweeter—in fine, where heaven is a little nearer. That spot of earth is one's own home. It is the presence of the mother there that consecrates it. It may not be especially attractive to others, but it is all the world to you.

The plantation selected for description here is the author's old home and the home of his forefathers for generations. Many in North Carolina, in breadth of acreage and varied attractiveness, may have been of greater marketable value and far more desirable. The author knows this best and thinks it a fair type of the old plantations of the South, and, therefore, for various reasons, it has been selected as the scene of the recitals, descriptions, events and conditions of life embodied in the life on Southern estates before the years of 1861 and '65. It is situated in the old county of Onslow, named for Sir Arthur Onslow, Speaker of the British House of Commons. The plantation was known as "The Rich Lands" and was situated immediately on the old stage-road which led from New Berne to Wilmington, two old colonial towns, about one hundred miles apart, in the tide water section of the blessed old State of North Carolina. This estate lay on the west side of a very remarkable stream known as New River, which had its source and outlet in the same county. From its mouth in the Atlantic Ocean up to a short distance from the village of Jacksonville, the county seat, the beautiful body of water, known as "the river," was, in truth, in breadth, in depth and other particulars very like an arm of the sea. Rarely, if ever, has the eye of man elsewhere drunk in the beauties of nature as so strikingly presented by this lovely estuary or bay. Something like it is to be seen along the St. Mary's River in lower Maryland. Some of the views of the Hudson remind you of it. All in all, however, the writer has never seen anything quite so beautiful. It was some twenty miles in length and several miles in breadth, with an expanse of water strikingly lovely.

One must take into consideration the fact that this beautiful body of salt water constituted the abundant storehouse of nature, from which were taken some of the most valued features of table comfort and luxury. Its waters teemed with the various varieties of fine fish found in this latitude, among which were the mullet, the sea trout, the sheep- head, the flounder, the croaker or pig fish, with others not a few. These fine fish were there in great abundance. In their season were to be had many varieties of water fowl, ducks, wild geese and swans. The ducks were very numerous and of the varieties found in that famous storehouse, the Chesapeake Bay. Never in this country has the writer tasted a more delicious breakfast dish than the blue winged teal of these waters, while the blackheads, mallards, and the variety, which we call the canvasback, were found in large numbers. Rich and abundant as were all these contributions to the planter's comfort, none surpassed the shellfish found so abundantly where this beautiful inland salt lake joined the sea. The oysters were larger and fatter than the celebrated "Blue Points" of the New York market, and in delicacy of flavor quite equaled the "Morris Cove" specimen of the Philadelphia Club House. The writer married a Virginia girl and has often feasted on the fine oysters of the Norfolk and Suffolk markets (and they are certainly very fine), but, apart from prejudice or predilection, he is free to say that the "New River" oyster of the old plantation days in all the finer forms of delicacy and flavor were the equals of any bivalves he has ever enjoyed. At Delmonico's in New York or at the old Hygeia at Old Point Comfort nothing of the oyster family surpassed them. The very largest and fattest oysters in the country are to be had in the Mobile and New Orleans' markets. These graced the beautiful tables of the old St. Charles and St. Louis of the latter city in the good old antebellum days; but, while they were as large as the hand of the Creole beauties at the table and as white with fat as the snowy arms of these beautiful women, they lacked the peculiar, dainty, salty flavor of the "New River" oyster. They were much larger, much fatter, this fruit of

39

the Gulf waters, but were far too fresh, lacking in saltiness, and this for a very obvious cause. The large inland seas, the Alabama and Mississippi rivers, poured such quantities of fresh water into the gulf as to lower the standard of saltiness of this oyster's habitat; but though in return they brought down such myriads upon myriads of animalcule as to make these oysters of the Gulf as long as an ordinary knife of the tea table, as broad as a man's four fingers and looking like great strips of white pork, yet they were not comparable in flavor to the New River oyster of the North Carolina markets. In addition to these toothsome oysters of this remarkable river, there was an inexhaustible supply of crabs, both stone and soft shell, while clams, scallops, and shrimp were to be had for the taking. In addition to the above named comforts, which, in the good old golden days before the war had become to the planters and their families actual indispensable necessaries, both the bathing and sailing were most excellent. The writer goes back in fond recollection to many sunny hours of the charming sailing or yachting parties over these beautiful waters, as fair and lovely as those in the Bay of Naples. In these we were often joined by the charming people of Col. Edward Montford's family or those from Paradise Point, in both of which such sweet hospitality obtained.

The soil along the shores of the lovely inland lake, while lacking in the greater fertility of the plantations higher up the river, was most kindly in many of the wise bestowments of nature, and the planters lived in great comfort and luxury. The strong, beating tidal pulse of old ocean had not the power to force its sway higher up New River than just below Jacksonville, the county seat. Here the tide ended. Higher up the river, narrowing rapidly, you came to some of the finest agricultural country in this State. In the center of this lovely section, on the west bank of the river, in the form of a horseshoe in the bend of this beautiful stream, lay the far-famed "Rich Lands" estate. As it lay there with its broad, fertile acreage, embellished here and there with the largest hickory trees the writer has ever seen, it stretched away on either side of the stage road running from Wilmington, fifty-eight miles away, to New Berne, just forty-two miles distant. This road, running from north-west to southeast in almost an airline for something over two miles, cuts this estate in two parts of almost equal extent. The writer loves to shut his eyes, close his ears, go back in fond memory, and think of it as the most beautiful plantation his eye ever feasted upon. Some of the estates in the Mohawk Valley are very lovely, and lovely homes on fine farms are to be seen in the far-famed Shenandoah Valley of Virginia.

The American may be justly proud of his country, capable of furnishing such landed estates as are to be seen in the blue-grass country of Kentucky and the more fertile sections of Alabama, in the canebrake country between the Alabama and Tombigbee Rivers. These are all very fine, as is that far-famed section of Bayou Teche in Louisiana. But this plantation of which we are speaking—in all the elements of fertility, lay of the land, readiness of renovation, variety of products, proximity to market, freedom from wasting diseases, the ease with which a fine table could be maintained winter and summer, the excellence of its roads, its inexhaustible forests of fine wood, hard and soft—in the judgment of those entitled by both education and travel to an opinion in such matters was, in the early fifties, under the management of the proprietor, the father of the present writer, one of the very finest estates in the South. The reader will concur, when we go into details. It embraced more than twenty-five hundred acres of arable land, while to the west and south, adjoining, there extended a magnificent domain of more than twenty thousand acres of heavily timbered land, comprising the turpentine orchards of this estate. The plantation proper was almost as level as a parlor floor, save where one beautiful stream, Chapel Run, cuts its way through the fields as it went on its way with sparkling waters to the river. The geological formation was that of limestone, not the hard, granite like, blue limestone of the Shenandoah valley; this was the softer gray limestone, easily

41

disintegrating, and from its rich percentage in the carbonate of lime, when applied, readily restoring fertility to the soil, reduced by heavy cropping. The beautiful stream spoken of, Chapel Run, fed by innumerable springs, some of them in view and others hid away in its banks and bed, was a bold, strong creek, spanned by several rustic bridges, ornamented by vines, which were a very great convenience in going to and from the plantation work, and notably so in harvesting the crops. Its headwaters were strong, unfailing springs, a little west of the plantation, out on the eastern fringe of the turpentine orchard. The writer, in boyhood, on Saturdays and other holidays was never so happy as when fishing in its glassy pools, as limpid as Lake Killarney in old Ireland. They abounded in small though very delicious fish of the perch family, commonly called pan or the breakfast fish of the planter's table.

Do you see that fine old beech tree standing on the bank of this stream, just before it disappears and goes into its subterranean channel, which some convulsion of nature has made for it? What a splendid old tree it is! How stately its trunk, how umbrageous its branches, how smooth its white bark? What rough, hieroglyphic signs are those, well-nigh grown over now, hut once cut deep into the soft bark of this lovely tree, as the young fisherman stopped his sport and with pocket knife engraved the following letters, "E. P. F.;" while higher up, the work of an older brother, could be read the unmistakable initial letters of one of dear old Carolina's beautiful daughters, "A. E. C. D." Thus we see that Cupid was busy then with the sons of the old planter. Those who wore the names outlined by those initials have passed away, but to him who alone survives, the younger brother, the present writer of these pages, their sweet memory will outlast the famous old beech tree and will go on with him into eternity, forever blessed. Do you see that large persimmon tree standing out there in the open field, some hundred yards or more from the banks of the creek? Yes; why do you ask the question? Because it has connected with it some high fun of possum hunting, with dear old Ben and his dogs, "Rattler" and "Spunk." Maybe it would be well to stop my plantation reminiscences for a little while and give you a sure enough possum story? What do you say? I do not know how the reader will like it. In these times of the bicycle and the fame of Newport and Narragansett Pier, times have so changed. Nevertheless, here goes for the possum story. Those who prefer to do so can skip it and indulge in reading one of Zola's elevating (?) stories.

On one of the Carolina plantations before the war lived an old darky named Hannibal, commonly known as "Uncle Han," whose proud fame as a possum hunter or a trapper was well known on the plantations on both sides of the river. He was very lucky with "varmints," as the Negroes said. On this particular occasion he had gone to his trap and found that it had been robbed, but he set it and carefully baited it and went to another trap higher up the creek. Here he was delighted to find he had caught a fine large animal, well fatted on persimmons, which the early frosts had mellowed and sweetened. In less time than is required to tell of it he had, with one blow of his axe, cut down a young ash and with the possum's tail held fast in the split of the stick, thrown over his shoulder, he was making his way home, to reach which he was obliged to pass by a little country store where whiskey was sold. Uncle Han's joy over the prospect of the oncoming feast was so great that he could not pass that store without stopping both to wet his whistle and to fill his "tickler." Thus supplied, homeward he went and, though it was late, he soon had the possum on a spit before a roaring fire. Now and then the old man would wet his whistle from the contents of that bottle. Soon, between the heat of the fire, the soothing influence of the whiskey and the day's work, he was deep down in an old split-bottomed chair, fast asleep. Aunt Rachel, his wife, had gone to bed sometime before. Still the old man slept on. A little blue-black Negro in the neighborhood, named Henry, worried the very life out of Uncle Han by robbing his traps, and other deviltries. He had gone to the old man's trap that very night and

43

saw from the hair still sticking to it that Uncle Han had been lucky. He followed on. He came to the old man's cabin and, through a crack in the wall, he took in the situation. There was the fat possum roasting away before the fire; there sat, or rather half way reclined, Uncle Han in his chair, pretty far gone from the effects of his frequent drinks, fast asleep. Henry's mouth was just watering for some of that possum, but still he waited. All was quiet as the grave, save an occasional snore from the old man. After a time when the odor of the roasted possum told the young darky that all things were ready, he softly opened the door, tiptoed to the fireplace, took down the possum, and at the table ate and ate and ate until fully satisfied; then, to add insult to injury, he took a little of the possum's fat and with his finger gently smeared it on the old man's lip, who was far gone with whiskey and sleep. Then the little blue-black imp of mischief went out of the house as quietly as he could and, taking a good-sized chunk of wood, he swung it high into the air, giving it such a turn that it came down with a tremendous *"k'bam"* on the old man's roof. It was a fearful noise in the dead of the night. The old man, fearfully startled from his sleep, sprang up from his chair, about half asleep and more than half drunk, and called out, "Hello! Hello! Rachel, old woman, whar's my possum?" and then, his tongue touching the possum fat on his lip and sucking it for its very savoriness, he began again, "It tas' like possum; it mus' be possum; it surely am possum. I'll tell yuh w'at's de truf 'bout dis, old woman, I mus' have eat dat possum in my sleep; but I tell yuh w'at's de fac', if I did, and I mus' hav' dun it, it lies li'ter on my stumac' and gives me less satisfacshun dan any possum eve' I eat befo' in all my born days." To which the old woman, Aunt Rachel, wisely replied. "Stop talkin' 'bout yo' possum, yuh ole fool yuh. Put out de lite an' com' to bed; it's mos' day and yuh is drunk, dat's what yuh is."

CHAPTER IV.

Hunting and fishing and other forms of fine fun and frolic on the old plantation.

ON either side of the stage road from Wilmington to New Berne, as it passed through the plantation, were well kept fences of the old-fashioned zigzag or Virginia style. In alternate corners of the fence were planted fruit trees, not of the short lived, modern, grafted, or budded varieties, but trees grown from seed in case of the peach and cherry, and from the scion where the apple tree was desired. The result was that the trees planted in the early part of the century in some cases were bearing fruit in the early forties. Here and there, as good taste or convenience might suggest, the stately black walnut and hickory and an occasional mulberry tree had been allowed to stand. Here and there, when in full foliage, the dark leaved persimmon trees were dotted about the twelve or thirteen fields into which this large plantation was divided. The theory of the proprietor was that as the stock congregated under these persimmon trees to eat the fruit their shade did not lessen the productiveness of the fields where they stood. Certainly, with their deep, dark green foliage and symmetrical outlines, they gave much beauty to the landscape. Grandfather and father in their holding of these ancestral acres, evinced much wisdom in guarding their lovely trees and protecting the forests from vandal waste. It would have been far better for the landed estates of the South if the timber, especially the hardwood, had been more carefully guarded and economized.

It was the custom of the proprietor to cultivate the fields on either side of the road on alternate years. At convenient distances from each other, large barns and cribs for the safe storage of the

45

crops had been built, surrounded ordinarily by broad shelters and enclosed sheds for the comfortable stabling of the cows and sheep at night and for the feeding of the horses and mules at noon in the busy months of the year. Some of these barns were old and so constructed as to allow a four or six mule team to drive in with grain or forage and, after the load had been deposited, to pass out through the opposite double door. Connected with these barn yards there were closely fenced stock yards for the better management of the cows, sheep, hogs and colts of the plantation. These were well furnished with pumps or wells, affording an ample supply of water for the stock, which, however, the servants were not allowed to drink, as they were strongly impregnated with limestone of such quality as to render the water unhealthy for man, but which the animals could drink with impunity. The water that the servants drank was brought out in large casks mounted on wheels and was served to them in gourds or calabashes from wooden cans made by the plantation coopers from cedar, cypress or juniper wood, with which the estate abounded. By subterranean sinks or natural wells in this limestone formation the fields were admirably drained and the ditches were comparatively inexpensive. As you approached the river, where the land was undulating, there were numerous marl beds which had been worked for many years, and which in their rich deposits yielded the much-desired lime for agricultural purposes. Some of them afforded in abundance a marine deposit as high as seventy-three per cent, in carbonate of lime, with traces of magnesia and phosphoric acid. If you examine this specimen carefully you will find parts of the skeletons of sea animals, fish, crabs, turtles, etc. These bones account for the rich phosphates contained in the marl.

"What crop of dark, rich green is that which you see along the western slope of those hills, and far out into the bottom of that two hundred acre field?"

"That is the far-famed black-eyed pea of the South, the substitute for clover, which the long, hot summers of the South preclude from the crops of this plantation."

"What noise is that we hear over in that direction?"

"That's the song of the boys on their light carts hauling the marl to be scattered broadcast over the crop of peas, which you see is just going into bloom, the height of its exuberance, when it will be turned under good and deep, with a sweep chain connected with the plow to force the peas down, so as to be reached by the plowshare. This is the preparation for the wheat crop. Yes, the proprietor, while not numbering wheat among the staples of his plantation, always produces enough for home consumption and his seed for the next year."

"What other crop is that growing down there just along the river bank?"

"That's our rice crop. You observe the acreage is not large and yet there is plenty and to spare for all the plantation requirements."

"What small birds are those rising up from the rice fields in such large numbers as to almost darken the view?"

"They are the famous rice birds of the South just now holding their high carnival, attacking the rice crop just as the grain is going into its milky state."

"What means that discharge of firearms, with reports so loud and long sustained as to suggest a body of infantry?"

"That's old Uncle Amos and his band of helpers shooting these birds to protect the crop from these dainty little enemies. Have you ever eaten a rice bird?"

"Not that I know of. I have eaten the sora or the reed bird, killed in the Valley of the Patuxent in Maryland, and it is certainly very delicious. So far as I know, it may be the famous ortolan.[5]"

---

[5] Esteemed as a table delicacy.

This conversation took place between the older son of the planter and his college mate from Princeton, a charming young gentleman from Maryland, who had come home with the young Carolinian to enjoy a week or two of hunting and fishing and other forms of fine fun and frolic on the old plantation.

"Wait until breakfast to-morrow," said my brother John, "and when you have eaten our rice bird, fat as butter, bones and all, you will never brag again of your sora,[6] of your ortolan, of your famous reed bird, for I tell you, Tom Bowie, that this bird of the Carolinas, fatted on rice in the milky state, is the most delicate, toothsome food I ever tasted."

"Let us now turn our faces homeward, for we have fully two miles to ride and the afternoon is far spent."

As these two young gentlemen, mounted on horseback, turned the heads of their horses away from the river they came up with an old Negro, "Uncle Daniel," riding in a cart drawn by a mule, well laden with corn in the ear. The old man is on his way to one of the feeding stations to give some twenty-five or thirty bullocks their evening meal. These are being fatted for the early winter markets, and had you time, reader, to inspect them closely you would find fine specimens of the Durham breed of cattle, of the large size and of admirable fattening properties, of which the proprietor was very proud.

"What is that more than half grown servant doing over there to the left of us?"

"We will ask him. Fred, what are you doing?"

"I'm penning the sheep, sah."

Yes, every night the flocks of sheep, of which there were several, numbering in all some three or four hundred, were carefully penned, for the double purpose of making manure in their well-littered folds, protecting the grown animals from the

---

[6] A small, short-billed rail, Porzana carolina, of marshy areas of North America.

48

ravages of the dogs, and from the fox's known fondness for the lambs of the flocks. As one comes from the plantation proper and crosses the creek, on ascending the hill on the south side one enters one of the most beautiful avenues of cedars in this section of the State. It stretches away to the gate leading into the large grounds surrounding the mansion and embracing its curtilage, in length some half-mile and breadth some forty feet, as level almost as a dining room table.

Who are those four, men—servants—we meet at the bow of the hill? Two of them are between fifty and sixty years of age, one is a shade older and the fourth is about thirty-five years old. The old man mounted on a blood bay mare, with black mane, tale and legs is Uncle Philip, the next in authority to the proprietor on the whole plantation. The youngest of the four is Cicero, the coachman. Observe him, if you please, as with all the air of a trained jockey he jauntily sits in the saddle. Did you ever see a more beautiful animal than that? You will not wonder when told that his dam was a Sir Archy mare, Vashti, the celebrated Tar River filly, and well known on the American turf. She "let down," or strained a tendon running against the famous old horse "Boston" on Long Island course. His sire was Trustee, the father of Fashion. The other two servants are Uncle Suwarro, named for a famous Russian general, and the trusted foreman of the plowmen of the plantation, while the small blue-black Negro is Uncle Jim, the foreman of the hoe force of the plantation. Why are they so much excited? The large bell on the estate has struck the hour of noon, and as it is Saturday everybody is called off from work till Monday. This has been the custom of the plantation for a long, long time. No work after twelve o'clock on Saturday, unless it be during the harvest season.

You observe those marl carters have all come in and there is an air of excitement on the faces of all the servants you see. What is up? There's a horse race on foot. Uncle Philip and Cicero are to try the speed of their respective horses and these two old foremen have come up the avenue to give them a fair start, while Robert, the blacksmith, holds the purse of ten dollars, which is the wager on this occasion. Harry and Ben are the judges. Presently you hear, in trumpet tones the word "Go," and off they speed along the whole length of the avenue, through the open gateway of the enclosure as rapidly as the horses can put their feet to the ground, both running under whip and spur. Cheer after cheer rends the air as Cicero's friends claim the victory, for the judges rule against old Uncle Philip, who yields as gracefully as he can, but who "cusses" a little and then rides in, puts up his horse, opens his little store and proceeds to gather in the six-pences and shillings, with which to make the purse for another race with that "skillet headed negur," Cicero, as in anger and contempt, the aristocratic old man calls his adversary of the plantation turf.

CHAPTER V.

A tour of the plantation great-house.

WE HAVE had a glimpse of the sports and pastimes of the servants in the ante-bellum days on this old estate. We have seen that there were joyous breaks in the days of labor, which made their plantation, not only an abode of much comfort but a scene of marked beauty in its well cultivated fields and other features of telling thrift. Before we go very far into the details of the lives of these dusky sons and daughters of toil, we shall devote an entire chapter to the amusements, in which the old planter encouraged them to indulge. We shall see with our own eyes that if the prosperity of the South was the natural result of systematized labor, one feature of the system was the recognition of the fact that the highest forms of usefulness and efficiency in life are only reached in the judicious unbending of the bow of labor. The question is often asked, "Is it not well-nigh as important that people in all the relations of life should be properly amused, as that they should be fed?" The institution of the various public games among the ancients answered this question to the satisfaction of the pagan mind, while the elaborate and painstaking opening up of the beautiful parks in our modern cities, with wide spreading groves and lovely views of miniature lakes with laughing cascades, all at great cost to the public, voices the wisdom of the nineteenth century civilization on this subject. Surely the old planter was wise in amusing as well as feeding and sheltering his servants.

Before going any deeper into this narrative, while yet we are on horseback, let us ride up this broad avenue of lovely elms and see what lies beyond. You observe it leaves the great public road just before you reach the large gate through which Uncle Philip and Cicero disappeared a moment ago at the close of the horse race. This avenue, some four hundred yards in length, is about forty feet in width and, leading due east, it gradually approaches the old mansion on the crest of an eminence. This gives the dwelling and its curtilage almost perfect drainage, so important in a flat or level country. As we ride along this avenue, on the left and right are two of the orchards of this estate, while still further on the right is a large number of buildings of various sizes and adapted to various uses. This large assemblage of houses is known as the "quarter," or the village, in which the homes of these many servants stand. But you see we are at the end of the avenue and just in front of us is the gate of the front yard of the writer's old home. Before entering it let us give up our horses to Cain and George who will take them to the stables for us. We can walk in now. Before doing so let us stop a moment or so and admire those fine trees, native to the soil, equidistant and at the same angle from the corners of the front piazza. Do you see those two noble old beech trees with trunks almost as large as a flour barrel and as symmetrical as if the then popular landscape gardener, Downing, had grown them to suit his beautiful taste? What monarchs they are and how comfortable the seats at their base, constructed of undressed hickory shoots. What splendid tree is that just at the front gate of the side yard sloping away to the little stream at the foot of the hill just north of where we stand? That is a pecan tree.

Let us stand there a moment or two and take in the outline of the planter's dwelling. You see it is a very large house. Yes, inclusive of the piazzas it is just sixty feet square, three stories high, built of the best North Carolina pine and weather boarded with fine yellow poplar. It stands on brick pillars about five feet above ground, with no suggestion of cellarage, so as to avoid every semblance of dampness. Why did not the old planter, with his abundant means, build it of brick? He is far too wise for that. In a damp climate brick is not the material for the construction of healthy homes. The planter's ancestry found that out to their deep sorrow long years ago, when in the settlement of New Berne, at the junction of the Neuse and Trent rivers, brick were employed for building purposes and many of the old Huguenot families suffered terribly, burying their dead from diseases incident to life in brick houses, in a damp, warm, malarial climate. So you see the house is of wood, but of such wood as the modern house builder never finds in these days. It is the very best of the original forests, carefully selected and seasoned in such manner as to preclude wind shakes, seams or cracks. The truth is these old planters, except in a fox hunt or deer chase, were not of the order of men to hurry about anything, and least of all in the selection of material in the construction of their fine old homes.

We must hurry up and describe this old mansion, for there are many things of interest to be told about it, and supper will be ready before you know it. Come, let us enter the old home. This piazza extending all around the house, first and second stories, is about twelve feet in breadth; and you observe the windows, of large size, open down to the floor. Well, the front door is wide open.

"Why do you lift your hat as you enter?"

"I do so in reverence of what I know is within."

"Yes, full right you are."

This old roof tree shelters the spot sacred to the very finest forms of old-fashioned Southern hospitality, the decadence of which we have witnessed to a saddening degree since 1865, but which still lingers here and there in the South; not, however, of the order which challenged the admiration of all who felt the touch of our lares and penates in the good old plantation days. The hallway, running the whole depth of the house, is very broad, and the two sets of stairways are correspondingly broad and of easy pitch or grade, to compensate in some degree for the modern elevator. You observe as you pass along the hall you are met by another hall just as broad, cutting the one by which we enter at right angles. Another feature of these broad halls is that

53

quite as much money is judiciously expended in furnishing them as in any other part of the old home, while hammock-hooks suggest an indefinable comfort of a hot day, and book shelves tell you that the old planter's life consisted not in "bread alone," but that books entered largely into the life on one of these noble old estates. Here and there, beside the hat or cloak stands of fine old mahogany, you observe the polished horns of the patriarchs of flock and herd fastened securely under the old pictures gracing the walls. As you just now entered the large folding front door to your right hand, through that heavy door of oak finish, you enter the large parlor, with its piano, violin and guitar cases, and such bestowment of fine taste and ample means, in rich old furniture, with oil paintings and costly carpets and rugs as you would expect to find in the planter's home. The south-east corner room was the bedchamber of my father and mother, while across the hall was the nursery, and opposite the parlor was the family living or sitting room. In the two stories above were the rooms peculiarly devoted to the comfort of the daughters of the planter and the guests of the family. The attic rooms were devoted to the storage of bed clothing, cedar chests for woolens, trunks and such other features of a well-appointed family. As you pass out of the large hall, running north and south across the broad piazza, you enter into another piazza in front of the large dining room opening back to one of the largest kitchens you would be likely to meet, with every convenience of closets for china and storerooms numerous and spacious.

Stop a moment. Look at that capacious kitchen fireplace, broad enough to take in logs of wood six feet long and with old-fashioned crane for swinging the large pots on and off, as the old cook might like, with its smooth hearth running the whole width of the chimney and back three or four feet into the room. Why is this hearth so broad? For two reasons. First, it guards against the danger of fire; secondly, on its broad area, in small ovens and tin kitchens, are carried to perfection some of the finest forms of good cooking of savory dishes for which this era of plantation life is .so justly celebrated. What hooks are those driven into the bricks just below the broad shelf or mantelpiece? They are employed when a wild turkey or a roast of venison are there cooked, basted meantime with vinegar and lard or butter, being constantly turned around so as to present no one side too long to the roaring fire as to burn the meat, while the metal dish underneath catches all the juices as they are distilled by the great heat from the roaring fire. What large block of wood is that standing between the windows on one side of the kitchen, about three feet in diameter and four feet high? That is where the old cook beats her famous biscuit, which are the most delightful of all breads. Defying and despising both baking powder and soda, the old-fashioned Southern beaten biscuit is the very nonpareil of breakfast or supper bread, equally good, hot or cold, in its flaky lightness. The French cooks of neither New York nor Paris have ever been able to equal it. In very truth it surpasses the famous Vienna rolls of the Washington City club houses. In their highest perfection they have sadly disappeared, with the old turbaned cooks of the old plantation regime, who mastered all their secrets. Later on we shall sample old Aunt Patty's beaten biscuit but we must hurry out of the kitchen, for we have much to see before we go down to the quarter.

Standing on the kitchen piazza and looking east to your left and in front, there is an area in form of a quadrangle about one hundred feet on each side. In the center of this area is a well of water, supplied with a pump, well sheltered and with vines of honeysuckle trained to the sides. What houses are those with broad shelters facing south and west on this area? These are the smoke houses, three in number, in which the hams of five hundred hogs are cured annually. Those other houses are what are called the flour house, the coffee house and the large storehouse for groceries, etc. In the rear of the smoke houses are smaller houses for the storage of potatoes and oysters in the shell. These delicious bivalves are kept in a dark room and are so well fed with meal stirred into salt water as to be scarcely able to stay in their shells. Unfortunately, however, they will lose their flavor after a few days, showing clearly that we cannot compete with nature. Just in the rear of these houses, on the brow of the hill, so as to be kept perfectly dry, are the various and spacious houses for poultry of all kinds, as well as the stately peacock, the strutting old turkey gobbler, the guinea fowl, the several varieties of ducks (the Muscovy, the Puddle and the English) and the ordinary barnyard fowl or chicken. They are all here in this yard of two acres or more, well fenced in, secure from the egg-sucking cur of the Negro quarter, as well as from mink or weasel at night.

Coming out of the poultry yard, let us go through the east gate of the area on which stands the large pump above described. To your left, through the gateway, let us enter and see if you ever saw a more beautifully appointed vegetable garden? In extent about an acre, it embraces in its various products all that you may wish to find, from the delicate tropical eggplant to the more commonplace cabbage. Here they all are. You need not wonder at the delicious vegetables found in such great abundance on the planter's table. Coming out of the garden what buildings are those off to the left? The first you see are the weaving rooms, in which are manufactured all the fabrics with which the servants of the plantation are clothed, including the woolen goods for winter and those of cotton for the summer. Those other houses you see down yonder, six in number, are where the house servants are quartered.

There live dear old Aunt Phebe and her husband, Uncle Daniel. In the next house live Cicero, the coachman, and his wife Eliza. In the next dwell Handy, the dining room servant, and the laundress, Jane, with her family of girls, who are maids to the young ladies. Off to the south of the mansion, and separated from it by a large flower garden, is an enclosure of two acres or more devoted to almost every variety of small fruit. Here were grown some of the very finest melons that ever graced a Southern breakfast table and the corn for the table that made such fine fritters.

A description of this old home would not be complete were you not told of the use to which that large enclosure west of the chicken yard is put. Why is the fence so high? Why are those pieces of timber driven so far down in the ground, the ends of which you see projecting? Come, go with me to the gate for a moment and we will see. Here they come—Staver, Nimrod, Fashion, Venus, Starlight, Little Jolly and all the twenty or more of splendid fox hounds—eager and anxious to dash by you and hurry away to the woods for the chase. Is not that a splendid Irish setter there? Did you ever see a more beautiful animal in your life than that coal black pointer, black as night except one white toe? Beautiful names they have—Inez for the pointer, Don for the setter. The tall fence and the spikes driven into the ground now explain themselves. This is the dog kennel, with all its appointments for comfort and health for one of the best packs of hounds found in North Carolina. Why does the old planter keep those fine bucks in the kennel with the dogs? It is to familiarize the dogs with sheep and thus prevent many a worry on the hunt. As we expect to follow these dogs in a fox chase we will now leave them and inquire for what purpose those comfortable looking cottages up there on the hill are put? They were built by the old planter when his sons became large enough to go out to parties at night, so that they would not disturb their mother when they came home late, often accompanied by their young friends. We might spend an hour or so very pleasantly in the old flower garden, looking at the rich products of the fine taste of the mistress in this department; but who is this coming up the walk with rather stately step and, as he approaches, greets the two young gentlemen as they come out of their offices? This is an A.M. of the University of Edinburgh, Scotland, and who afterwards stood conspicuous among the Presbyterian divines of the State, as well for his broad learning as his deep spirituality. Would you know his name? This is the Rev. James Melsey Sprunt, as fine a type of a man, intellectually and morally, as ever-blessed two young Southerners in the capacity of tutor.

Before this volume is finished we hope to see him again, as he sits around the hearthstone of the old home of a winter's night and with kindling eye and the sweetest of voices reads aloud Shakespeare, the Waverley novels, Dickens, Bulwer, and others authors of worldwide fame.

CHAPTER VI.

"Bird's-eye" view of the plantation.

THUS you have had a bird's-eye view of the planter's home, so far as that portion in which he lived is concerned. Let us go down to the quarter and both inspect and describe the buildings in which the servants lived, and then we shall the more intelligently observe what fine specimens of health are presented by both the men and women of this estate. But you appear to be fatigued and maybe we had better defer this until Monday, for tomorrow will be Sunday, and the old planter insists upon everybody going to church? We will go in presently and enjoy the evening breeze on the south piazza as it comes from the sea, for, though in an airline we are some twenty miles from the ocean, regularly at this season of the year we get the cool, moist breeze, with its salty taste, as God sends it to us, by His great laws which govern the winds and the tides. The horses are ordered for 10:30 to-morrow morning (you said you preferred the saddle to the carriage, did you not?) and now for a little chat on the piazza and our supper, and then some music or, if you prefer it, we will ride over and see if those girls came up from Wilmington to the neighboring plantation.

Just then a gentleman some fifty-five years of age made" his appearance. You cannot mistake him. The age and the conditions which produced him have passed away, and yet he lives in the memory of all who have ever seen him. This particular representative of that noble type of Southern life; the old-fashioned country gentleman, was somewhat above the average height and size, about five feet eleven inches tall and weighing some hundred and sixty-five. He was not strikingly handsome, but with the class of face suggested by that of the old German

Field Marshal Von Moltke. With an ease of manner betokening gentle breeding, his marked characteristic was that peculiar type of manliness which came to a long line of progenitors living much in the open air. It was singularly attractive. His voice was that peculiar to the genuine sons of the South, soft, yet strong and singularly flexible, with marked emphasis given to the softer vowel sounds. His hair, originally jet black, was now tinged with gray, and from the large, soft blue eyes there was an expression of such tenderness as you always associate with a devoted husband and kind father. There was a compression of the lip, indicative of much will power, while the other features betokened the presence of so much that was notable and lovable, it would ever warrant one in thinking of this old planter as of such fine stamp, that while—

"His enemy could do no right, his friend could do no wrong."

Nearby him sat his other half, the blessed woman whom he had led from the neighboring county to grace his home and bless his life with that more than talismanic power which God has given to women in the bestowment of that far-reaching unselfishness which is constantly suggesting the Virgin's Son, and which is at once the source and secret of her strength and influence. Married in the early part of the century, so close and happy had been their married life that the blessed work of mutual assimilation had gone on to such a degree, that in many respects they were strikingly alike. To this marriage came the gift of nine children, four of whom had died in infancy or early childhood, leaving now two sons, the present writer and an older brother, and three daughters. The oldest daughter had married a Wilmington gentleman, gave birth to a lovely little girl and then fell asleep, when we placed her in the "God's Acre" of her fathers. Soon thereafter the second sister married Dr. W. W. D. of Wilmington, and leaving two sons, went into the Great Beyond to join her loved ones in the Paradise of God. But this is not a volume of genealogy. The above family events have been given in order that in proper connection may be stated a peculiarity of the old planter. One of the conditions of the marriage of these daughters was that the husband was not to take the wife away from the old home. The dear old father said, with telling pathos, that the family was too small, the acreage on the estate was far too great, and that the old mansion was far too large to allow of any colonizing. So we all dwelt there together, with cares, duties and responsibilities so divided out as to suggest the presence of no drone in the large hive.

But it is the supper bell we hear and after this meal, you remember, it was suggested that we should ride over to the neighboring plantation and see the girls of the old planter. We shall not describe this charming meal, because in another chapter we are to tell at length of the cookery, both in the great house and in the cabin. All went the next day and heard a most excellent sermon, in the commodious church, so arranged as to allow the presence of a large number of the servants. You would have been delighted to have seen how smart and tidy these servants were, as they appeared in their part of the church building, dressed up in their Sunday go-to-meeting clothes, reverently kneeling to worship that God, unknown to the poor pagans in Africa from which their fathers came. Sunday afternoon was passed in various ways. Some of the servants interchanged visits on the home plantation, or, furnished with written permits, went to see their friends on the neighboring estates. Some went out to the lake to bathe, riding the horses they worked during the week, in order to give both themselves and the horses a good bath in this beautiful sheet of limpid water. Ten o'clock at night found all of this large family comfortably established at home, ready for the refreshment of a night's healthy sleep, except those men servants who had married on the adjoining plantations, where they had gone on Saturday afternoon. These came in time for the assembly call, rung about sunrise on Monday morning.

We will get the most satisfactory view of the quarter by beginning at the east end of the principal street and, as we go along, carefully observing right and left. This street the Negroes called Broadway, and broad it was sure enough, as in width about seventy feet it ran almost due east and west for a long distance. The houses, separated about fifty feet from each other, were built up some distance from the driveway, with footpaths running along in front of them. Some of these were of cypress logs closely joined together and made perfectly tight with mortar, with hog or cow hair worked in it to make it stick in the crevices. They varied in size, as did the frame houses which were scattered here and there; the larger ones were given to the larger families for greater comfort and healthfulness. In size the average house was about thirty feet in length by twenty-two in breadth, and was divided into two rooms downstairs—one the cooking and living room, the other the family sleeping room—while the upstairs was similarly divided. Nearly all of these were furnished with good brick chimneys and ample fireplaces. In warm weather the cooking was done out of doors under an improvised bush shelter. Frequently both the front and the back of the houses were protected by shelters wider far, and, for their purposes, a great deal more comfortable than the modern veranda. In the rear of the house was the family back yard, with its henhouse and its plot of ground for a garden, with which each home was supplied. The provident families were never without vegetables, and notably so did the long stalked member of the cabbage family known as the "collard" abound, which, when well frosted, was both esculent and savory to their appetites, well whetted by a life in the open air and its perfect freedom from care and responsibility—those twin murderers of happiness in human life.

Come, go in one of the cabins, as many will insist on calling the homes of the servants on the old plantation. You will see they differ among themselves. Some are as neat and tidy as the wife and mother who meets you at the door and with graceful courtesy and kindly greeting invites you in; respectfully, yet warmly, inquiring about the white folks at the "great house—Ole Marster and Mistiss and Marse John and Marse Jeems and Miss Car'line." If you go in the sleeping room you will find that the prevailing bed is made of the long gray Spanish moss, with which the swamps to the east of the plantation abound. This moss they boil and pick with their fingers, stuffing their bed-ticks with it, so as to make a soft and springy bed. They draw their quota of blankets every winter from the plantation stores and, what with their quilts and comforters, which they make themselves, and the abundance of excellent firewood, there is no suffering from cold, such as comes to mind when you think of the white tenement sufferers in New York and other large cities. It is not stated that there are equal comfort and cleanliness in all these forty homes and more. Some of these servants are constitutionally neat and thrifty; others again will discover, in many ways, the fact that their mothers and fathers taught them by example to neglect order, system and the laws of cleanliness.

In the matter of health and consequent usefulness the planter, through his foreman, insisted upon a rigid police of each house every week, with such penalties as in his judgment conduced to a high standard of cleanliness and health, as well in the house as about the clothing. In the center of these buildings and just in the middle of the broad street, at the point of junction with a cross street, was the town well, with abundant supply of potable water. The streets were well shaded by long rows of fine elms and maples, while in the back yard is grown in many cases, the mulberry tree, whose abundant supply of fruit is so useful to Aunt Polly in feeding her chickens and ducks; nor is it despised by her children.

There are two or three features about the quarter of which mention must be made. In the garden of each one of these homes is a pig pen, in which two fine hogs are raised each year by the most thrifty of the servants. Where do they get the grain with which to raise and fatten these pigs? The head of nearly every family has his patch of ground, in which he grows corn, peas and

63

cotton, or any crop he prefers. When does he work his crop? On Saturday afternoon or by moonlight, if he likes to do so, instead of going coon hunting. So you see, that Sambo, drawing his rations, has meat to sell, and "Ole Marster" always allows him to take his "crap" to town in the large wagons, which invariably go to New Berne just before Christmas to do the plantation trading. Besides this, the old planter always stands ready to purchase anything marketable—eggs, chickens, ducks and wild fruit (whortleberries and currants) with which the woods abound in their season. You must not think for one moment that all the servants on the old plantation have all these things to sell. They do not. Only the thrifty ones; and the rule was, almost without exception, that those who were most faithful in the performance of plantation duties were industrious and frugal in their own little matters.

Let us speak of the laws of sanitation, which were rigidly enforced. Twice each year these homes, inside and outside, were carefully whitewashed. Once each week the yards were carefully inspected and all rubbish and garbage, under penalty, were placed on that compost heap you see there near the garden fence, heavily covered with marl, rich in lime, to decompose or sweeten any putrescent matter and thus keep the premises seemly and healthy. Again, do you see those oblong iron depositories, mounted on posts, enclosed in boxes, filled with earth along the sides and underneath? What are they and to what purpose are they given? Those large, iron troughs, six feet and more in length, four feet wide and some ten inches in height, are the old salt vats employed in the making of salt, by evaporation of sea water in the War of 1812, when the British embargo closed our ports to the West India salt. The old planter has purchased a number of them and mounted them as you see. They are filled with the resinous residuum from his turpentine distilleries, commonly known as dross, every afternoon during the sickly or malarial season: and when set to blazing, as they are every evening about twilight, three purposes are served. First, they

64

flood the village or quarter with strong light; secondly, they infuse the fumes of cooking turpentine in the air and thus purify it; thirdly, they destroy myriads upon myriads of mosquitoes and thus sweeten the sleep of these dusky toilers. You observe they are placed all along the streets and four of them are seen, two in front and two in the rear of the mansion. It was indeed a beautiful sight, that of these burning masses all ablaze at once, lighting up the truth of the old planter's love for his children and his servants in thus protecting their health.

You observe that especially comfortable looking house, just across the street from where we are standing, and the other next to it? Those are the homes of two of the foremen on the plantation; Uncle Jim with his wife, Aunt Patty, live in one, and Uncle Suwarro and Aunt Rachel occupy the other, with their respective families. What is that suspended high up in the air, just there between those two houses? That is the old plantation bell which, in the hands of Uncle Jim, regulates the movements of the servants, calling them to and from labor and telling out the hours for the various duties. Whose cabin or home is that just behind that large tree—"Pride of China," I think you call the variety? That is Granddaddy Cain's home and where his wife, my dear old "Mammy Phillis," lives. The old man you see there in the shade of the tree, hackling corn shucks for mattresses, is the patriarch of the whole plantation. He is quite old, but as he gets up and walks towards the door of his house and takes a drink of water out of a gourd, do you observe what a splendid specimen of a man he is—how tall? How magnificently developed in his heyday he must have been! When younger he was the plantation miller for many years, and for honesty and fidelity there was no servant on all the river estates whose reputation was more enviable. His word was as good as his bond, and no man of all the thousands who during the long years of his service brought grain to my grandfather's mill ever suspected him of dishonesty on either side. In his old age he is now one of the several stock feeders on the estate, and you can see him presently as he goes

65

down to the barnyard to get out his mule and cart and starts out to salt the cattle and feed the mares and colts. He is a devoted member of the Methodist Church, as many of the servants are. He holds his family prayers night and morning, rejoicing with many others in the hope of eternal life through the Blessed Nazarene. When the present writer was a boy he heard a good joke on the old man, illustrating his racial fondness for possum. This is the plantation version as given by my *factotum*,[7] Cain, his grandson.

"You sees, suh, dat granddaddy was a-holdin' his family prayers one nite, arter he done swung up a mity big fat possum fo' de fiah. It was Sa'ddy nite, suh, an' de possum was a-roastin' for the Sunday dinner. De ole man he prayed and he prayed, suh, 'til I thought he neber was gwine to quit; and he prayed on and he prayed on. All of a sudden he stopped rite short and he snuffed de air and called out, 'Philis, ole woman, sure's yuh is bawn dat possum is a-burnin' up. Why doan' yuh turn dat possum, ole woman, and dat mi'ty quick.' An' he went on a-prayin' and arter a while, suh, he busted out 'amen!' Surely, Marse Jeems, I wuz mi'ty glad to hear him say amen, for I was mi'ty tired, suh; but I was afeard to go to sleep, fur if I had I knowed granddaddy would have wore me out to a frazzle.[8] He was dat 'ticular, suh, of his prayer. Suah as you is born, Marse Jeems, he duz love possum all de same."

We shall hope to see Granddaddy Cain again before this volume closes—this *Fidus Achates*[9] of the old plantation.

---

[7] Handyman

[8] Spanked him.

CHAPTER VII.

The plantation — a place of "plenty."

LET US take this cross street, running out of Broadway into what the servants call Chestnut Street. What strikingly large building is that which fronts us as we go on in our rambling walk of observation? That is what is called, in the parlance of the plantation, the gin house or the cotton gin. You observe it is very large and three stories in height. To what use is it to be put? You see it is surrounded on all sides by a deep shedding; in this first shed room are kept the large family carriage, sulky, buggies and light wagons, some from the celebrated factory of Cook in New Haven, Connecticut, and several others from Dunlap in Philadelphia. The old planter prided himself on the cost and elegance of his vehicles, and that beautiful family carriage, finished in silk, did not cost him less than a thousand dollars, with fine, silver-plated harness to correspond. With the large, steel-gray horses purchased in Baltimore it makes up an outfit so exactly suited to her taste that the mistress would not take twenty-five hundred dollars for it. There is a well-appointed harness room, some of the very best of Concord, New Hampshire, work. Ah, these old planters and their families had the very best the markets of the world could afford. The large shed room on the east is known as the pork house, where the meat rations of the estate are kept, at the great doorway of which they are served or dealt out by weight on alternate Saturday afternoons. On the north side of the main building, in a commodious well lighted shed room, is where the carpenters, four in number, ply their most useful industries. On the west side you have two rooms, one in which Virgil, the painter, keeps his paints and oils; the other is where the various stores of hardware, nails, bolts, screws, etc., are kept. What octagon-shaped house is that out in the yard? That is the cotton screw or compress, where the cotton and wool are baled for market. That stairway out there to your left leads up to where the cotton is kept before it is ginned, and that small room there is where old Santy mends the harness, and half-soles the shoes of the servants. You observe in it the only stove on the estate? Why is this? This stove is used to keep the old cobbler's wax ends so warmed as to be pliable in the coldest of weather. You see, in the various and multiform appointments of his large estate, the old planter does not forget anything. Well, we must go on. What buildings are those down there in that little ravine, with the large gum trees growing nearby and those beautiful willows fed by the moisture of the small streams, which constitutes the drainage of the quarter? These are the quarters of perhaps the most useful and at the same time the most interesting servant on the estate; that is Robert, the blacksmith, and that Hercules of a man nearby is Washington, who wields the ponderous sledge hammer as though it were a toy. Look at the splendid muscle in those brawny arms, as he and his chief are keeping time with their hammers on the blazing iron on the anvil. Indeed it is an anvil chorus, and how the sparks do fly all over the smithy, but they are well protected by their ample leather aprons. What is Robert doing now? He is putting a set of steel plates on that beautiful saddle horse out there in the yard. Does he work in steel too? Yes, he served his apprenticeship when a youth under one of the best artisans in the city of Richmond, Virginia. So you see there is skilled labor on this estate as well as in Lowell, Massachusetts. That large room on the left is where Caesar, the wheelwright, makes and repairs the carts and wagons. As we ascend the hill from this ravine, on that broad level are many houses. To what uses are they put? Some of them are barns and cribs for the storage of grain and forage; others again are large wagon sheds and others still for the comfortable stabling of one hundred and fifty horses and mules that are required on this estate. Those out there are for the comfort of the milch cows and the five yoke of oxen. Over there in a more modern building are kept the fancy or pleasure horses of the family, while lower down, in a separate lot or enclosure with high fence all around, are the stables for the two fine stallions, "John Richlands" and Crackaway," the latter a valuable present from one of the old planter's dearest friends, William B. Meares, Esquire, of Wilmington; the former the colt of Vashti, the celebrated Sir Archy mare sired by imported Trustee, the father of the world-renowned Fashion, the empress of the American turf. Do you hear that fearful noise down there —a sort of combine of foghorn and trombone? My sakes! what an unearthly racket that is! It's the bray of old "Dosy," the jack, sire of many of the best mules on the plantation. Do you suppose the notes of Balaam's animal were either as deep or long drawn out? Never. The seer would have been deaf as well as blind in the angelic interview. But the disciples of the higher criticism must answer your questions satisfactorily on this point. Whose quarters are those in the center of the quadrangle on which faces so many of these buildings? Those are rooms known as the storehouse, in one of which dear old Ben sleeps, and in which are kept the saddles and bridles, the riding outfit of the family. How complete this saddlery is! Where does it come from? Mostly from the fine shops of Nashville, Tennessee, and one or two there are of the English Shafter pattern, bearing the London trademark. In this other larger room are kept the shoes, blankets and hats not yet distributed to the servants, while back in there you will find hoes of various patterns, from the narrow bladed rice hoe to the broader cotton hoe, rakes, shovels, axes, pickaxes, spades, pitchforks, wagon whips, collars large and small for horses and mules. What small room is that with long table and drawers, well supplied with hooks inserted in the wall. That is Ben's inner sanctuary or where the keys of the whole plantation, on both sides of the creek, are securely kept under his faithful eye. It would try our patience to stop long enough to count them all, but this faithful, honest darky knows and keeps them all in his safe

71

custody, while he is always ready to saddle you a horse if you wish to ride out on horseback, or on that long bench cut a ham string for Suwarro's use among the plowmen. We shall see Ben again before our work is done, for you must know him better. He is the embodiment of honesty with some of the queer African freaks, in its racial fondness for dress of bright coloring and fancy materials. In other words, Ben is the dude of the plantation, the Beau Brummel of his race, and so you will pronounce when you see him dressed up in his best bib and tucker for the plantation Christmas dinner, the description of which is yet before us. Dear old Ben! Blessed old Ben! He is gone long ago where the good darkies go! How the writer wishes he had a good likeness of him with which to embellish these pages, for a nobler spirit never breathed the breath of life. Across the river of life in the Great Beyond, Ben, I wave my hand to you; yes, I kiss my hand to you and hope soon to have long, long talks with you of the good old plantation days, when we will thank God that my people taught your people to know and love the Christ, the King.

There are some other things before us and we must hurry on. Let us go back to the old mansion, and in the description, which we would, leave of it let us insert two or three features of the outhouses, and just one on the interior of the house. Let us go upstairs and on the back piazza, which you observe is without roof, and see what Edith and Kate, the maidservants of the writer's sisters, are doing. They are helping Handy, the dining room servant, to bring up large trays of fruit—peaches, pears and apples—to be dried up there, where nothing will disturb them in the hot rays of the sun. What fruit is that of deep blood color? That is the wild plum of the plantation and those trays over there are full of whortleberries and wild currants. All of this wild or uncultivated fruit has been purchased from the young servants of the estate, gathered by them in the adjoining woodland stretching far away to the south. The storeroom was thus well supplied with delicious dried fruit, and in the winter pies, tarts and dumplings came in as a part of the dessert. As we go downstairs in the hall near the old planter's bedroom door what large enclosure of black walnut is that so like a handsomely finished wardrobe? That is the gun case or closet. Let us look in. Do you see that large double-barreled gun in the center there? That is the gun from a London manufactory (not Joe Manton's, but of very fine workmanship) and, you observe, heavily mounted with silver, with two sets of barrels to the same stock, a larger set for the larger game of bear and deer, while the smaller is used for wild turkey, partridges, squirrels and other smaller game. This is the planter's special property, while in the half-dozen other guns you will find such as will please almost any one, likely to use them. Besides the shotguns, there are two or three rifles of different calibre, and one other gun of large bore and great weight manufactured at the United States arsenal, in Fayetteville, North Carolina, and especially adapted to plantation purposes.

On the line of the fence dividing the poultry yard from the dog kennel, on the slope of the hill, do you observe that brick house partly embedded in the hillside? That is the most complete dairy or springhouse in this section of the State. Take down that calabash or gourd and dip down into that deep basin of crystal water that wells up in the center. No limestone there. Pure freestone or soft water and deliriously cool and very potable. Those troughs all around the sides of the dark, cool room are for the pans of milk. Let us count them. One, two, three and so on to twenty-four pans of milk. How yellow and rich it looks while the cream is coming to the top. Here come the milkmaids now. Do you observe, as they come through the side gate en route to the dairy, with what ease and apparently with what security they balance those large milk pails filled with milk, on their heads and without touching them with their hands? What is the secret of their ability to do this? Perfect health and strength, with long training from childhood up, running through generations, it may be from the jungles of Africa.

"How many cows are you now milking, Aunt Abby?" "'Bout twenty-five, suh." "What do your cows eat now?" "Dey's on the second crop of rice now, suh." Thus with twenty-five cows to milk and those fed on the second growth of the rice field, after the crop has been harvested, you will quite understand both the quantity and quality of the milk and butter which graced the old planter's table.

The object of the proprietor of this estate was to produce, as nearly as possible, everything consumed, as well on the plantation proper, as in the turpentine orchards. Thus the large number of casks of spirits of turpentine, as well as the thousands of barrels of resin, which were sold each year in the New York market, produced the monied income of the estate. The ordinary yield of corn was about thirty-five hundred barrels, with a large quantity of forage in fodder belonging to this crop, and they were nearly all consumed on the estate. Aside from the large number of beeves butchered on the estate, there were annually a large number sent to the market, while five hundred hogs every winter went to the shambles, providing the meat rations of the whole plantation. These furnished a supply of hams for the planter's table, in number so great that they went over from year to year, so that on a high day or a holiday it was not an unusual thing to have a ham on the table seven years old. The writer is entitled to an opinion on the subject of hams, and he here ventures to say that not even the Smithfield ham of Virginia nor that of Westphalia in Europe surpasses those which found their deep russet color in the green hickory and corncob smoke of the old plantation smokehouse. The flocks of sheep, both those on the plantation proper and those under the care of the white tenants in the turpentine orchards, yielded a fine supply of lambs in the spring of the year to go with the green peas of the early garden, with plenty of mutton throughout the year; while in the wool, both for home use and the markets, there was no little profit.

74

Just here let it be observed that among those ill-informed upon subjects upon which they do no little talking, and but little well informed thinking, the idea is common that there was little or no care taken in the selection of the breeds of farm animals on the Southern estates. It is true that the "razor-backed" hog was seen running at large and sometimes as wild as the country in which they were found. At the same time, on this estate and many others there were several improved breeds of swine, the Essex, the Poland China, the Jersey Reds, the Little Guinea, the Chester Whites, and that perfection of a farm animal of its kind, the Berkshire. The proprietor gave particular attention to the breeding of the Merino and Southdown sheep, while among his herds of cattle could be found as fine specimens of Durham and Devon breeds as one might care to see. This you must remember was before the introduction of the Alderney, Jersey or Guernsey from those small islands of England.

Among other products of this estate were large crops of the black-eyed pea, that Southern substitute for clover, and with this advantage to the pea, in that it was both grain and forage; some eighty or a hundred bags of cotton, with rice, tobacco and sorghum for home use. One can quite understand that when all the crops of this estate had been carefully harvested and the hog-killing or butchering season was over, with the era of "hog and hominy" fairly ushered in, there was a reign of such an abundance of good things as demanded with full warrant the observance of Christmas, that blessed queen of all the plantation high days and holidays, to which justice in nowise could be done until at least a full week had been allowed for this high tide of enjoyment, in both great house and cabin, to expend its force, finding its ebb on January second, when all entered on the duties of the new year. You may be upon the point of asking what were the rations of food and clothing, which went regularly to the servants on this estate, and of what did the rations consist? You shall have the answer. These people worked faithfully and they should have been warmly clad and abundantly fed. And so they

75

were. The rations were issued by weight on alternate Saturday afternoons. To each servant there was issued for these fourteen days a half bushel of cornmeal and seven pounds of the very best mess pork, with his potatoes, rice and sorghum, together with his twist or roll of tobacco. The bread ration was often not drawn, but the money equivalent paid at market rates, which ordinarily were fifty cents for meal and forty cents per bushel of potatoes. The clothing was all spun, woven, and made on the plantation. The work by which this was done was the outcome of the most perfect system in any department of the plantation industries. The hum of the spinning wheel, the noise of the loom, with the stirring whiz of the weaver's shuttle (all accompanied, many times, by the melody of plantation songs) "Way Down on de Suwannee River," "Carry Mo Back to Ole Verginny," "Massa's in de Cole, Cole Ground'" and many others which will grow into eternity with blessed memory as the writer crosses over and meets his dear sable friends, could be heard from January to December.

The clothing of so many servants required a great deal of systematized labor. The dyeing process was simple. The barks from the forest trees, the red oak, the poplar and dogwood, furnished the coloring, which was carefully set or fixed by old Aunt Daphne, by the judicious use of copperas and alum. This gave a serviceable brownish gray which rarely faded either in the woolen or cotton goods. Those bright red bars, about the width of your little finger, in the dresses of the young women and girls you see there fitting them so snugly, are the outcome of cochineal, known as "de turkey red" (and red it was) which gives delight to African eyes—just as scarlet as that seen in the uniform of the British soldier of revolutionary days in '76 and thereabouts. To each servant were allowed three full suits of clothes annually, with plenty of wool and cotton allowed the wives and mothers for as many pairs of socks and stockings as they required. Three pairs of shoes, one pair of blankets, one wool and one straw hat went annually with each ration. To those who were much exposed to bad weather, such as the drivers of the mule teams and ox-carts, warm overcoats, often weather-proof, were issued. The men employed in ditching, and Uncle Amos, who did nothing but hunt and "destroy varmints" from year's end to year's end (making the best wages of any servant on the estate, because he killed so many eagles, coons and an occasional bear, with untold numbers of squirrels, black and red fox and the gray or cat squirrel), were given heavy brogan boots. The hides and skins from the sheep and cattle slaughtered during the year were exchanged for shoes and the leather needed for harness purposes by Brown & De Rossett, the commission merchants in New York, to whom was also consigned the wool for which in exchange we received hats and blankets.

Thus cared for, we greatly doubt whether any European peasantry or the lower element, the farm laborers of England's population, or any factory element of either Old or New England fared as well as did the servants employed on this Southern plantation, under the practical, judicious and humane system which has been outlined on these pages. In maintaining this proposition I indulge in no misleading theories or distempered speculation. I discard the vaporing of all sickly, maudlin sentimentality when I say that no laboring population was ever better housed, better fed, better clothed or more humanely employed, as a rule (in which self-interest asserted itself, and where does it not assert itself?) than were the servants on this old estate of my father's. Would you ask what there is to justify this assertion? The answer is close at hand. Facts substantiated by figures. Statistics. You say that statistics are misleading. Yes. One can lie by figures, as seen in watered stocks in Wall street and elsewhere, but figures of themselves will not lie.

The rapidity with which the servants on the Southern plantation increased in number, say from 1810 to 1860, just a half century, for the sake of round numbers, is proof conclusive that the general laws of health must have been in the main largely obeyed, and the conditions of numerical increase in families must have been complied with, else the several hundreds of thousands of dusky forms of African laborers, at the close of the first decade of this century would not have grown into the millions which we all know were found south of the Susquehanna in 1865. From a general statement let us pass to a specific, well emphasized demonstration of the truth in this matter. On this plantation dwelt two married couples—Henry with his wife, Daphne, and George with his wife, Emelene. They must have been married in the late twenties. To the former couple were born thirteen children, boys and girls, twelve of whom they reared to full adult age. To the latter were born eleven children, of whom ten reached manhood and womanhood. In other words the increase of twenty-two servants from the parentage of four persons. This is an increase of more than four hundred per cent., and tells us its own story of kind treatment. Nor have we any ground for saying that these were exceptional cases, when we remember that to-day in the South there are whole Congressional districts in which the Negroes far outnumber the whites. Nor yet can anyone (save he who has been misled by Mrs. Stowe's ex parte, and therefore unfair, statement in "Uncle Tom's Cabin") say that the recital of facts, figures and conditions on these pages is not a fair picture of the old plantation life. Doubtless in Virginia on the James River estates, in South Carolina on the Wade Hampton plantations, and elsewhere in the South, there were many instances of even more humane treatment of the servants than is given here.

But we will go into no elaborate argumentation. The day for that is over. What we want are facts, and we are meeting Mrs. Stowe's statement, not by argument, but "by cool, dispassionate facts. What do you say to the portrayal of an element of African character in the form of an anecdote? Nothing pleases me more.

Well, it was a week of Christmas. Of several large gobblers, already fat, which had been put up in the large fattening coop to be flavored by the peanuts so abundant, one was missed. It created quite a stir. Handy, who fed the poultry, was excited, half mad and half frightened, in view of the consequences. Report was made to Uncle Jim, Suwarro and Ben, and close search was had. At last, so close was the search for the fine gobbler which was to grace "ole Marsteris" Christmas dinner table that he was found hid away in old Cupid's ash barrel. Report was made and arrest ensued, with incriminating facts. The old darky sent for his Marse John. His young master appearing, the following conversation ensued:

"Come, now, Uncle Cupid, tell the truth about it; the whole truth, mind you, old man, and nothing but the truth. Are you sorry or not that you stole that turkey?"

The old darky's racial fondness for turkey going into the background, under the shadow of his fear of penalty and in his great confidence in his young master, he called out:

"Marse John, you ax fo' de truf, doan' yo'?"

"Yes, Uncle Cupid, the whole truth."

"Well, now, suh, yo' see I can't say so mi'ty much 'bout bein' so 'ticular sorry I tuk dat turkey; but 'fore God, suh, young marster, I'se mi'ty sorry I was co'ch."

"That will do, Ben, let him go, he has told the truth. Don't steal any more turkeys, old man. Go home, now, and I will always stand by you when you tell the truth, for you certainly have told the truth this time—not so very sorry you took the master's turkey, but mighty sorry you were caught."

With loving laughter in his old eyes, Cupid went on to his home rejoicing, while Ben and the other servants laughed most heartily at the old man's straightforward honesty of speech, if not of act.

CHAPTER VIII.

Natural resources of North Carolina. Descriptions of various servants.

AS WE are about to enter on the description of the forest wealth of this estate—the turpentine orchards of the plantation, on which was expended by far the larger part of the labor and from which the revenue was mainly derived—it will be well if we pause just long enough here to make the full acquaintance of Uncle Philip, the manager of this department. In many respects, he was the most remarkable person of his class the writer has ever known. He was now about sixty years of age, of small stature, a genuine blue-black, as active as a boy of seventeen, and as quick in his motions as the beautiful horse Selim, which he rode. This animal was the joy and pride of the old man's heart, and ranked next in the old African's affection to his old master, for whom he bore a love which was the outcome of a close relation running through their lives. Philip had come down with the plantation from the planter's father. In childhood and boyhood, and in fact thus far in life, they had really been boon companions, together learning to swim, to ride, to handle firearms, and thus learning to know and to trust each other in a way and to a degree that few persons, if any, thinking of the institution of which their close relation was the product, can at this late day quite understand.

To both Fred Douglas and Booker Washington, in point of advantage given them by education, this noble old servant must necessarily have yielded; but he was very little, if any, inferior to any man, white or colored, the writer has ever known, in all that is understood by keen active mother wit and strong common (or rather uncommon) sense. Outside of his small family there was no one of a very large acquaintance whom the old planter loved more tenderly or trusted more implicitly. Thoroughly illiterate, really not knowing a letter in the book, he was fully equal to all the details of his large and important trust. His memory, naturally strong and tenacious, by constant use and honest trust in it, served him instead of memoranda, and his verbal report of the week's work which went on the plantation books regularly every Saturday afternoon, was both full and accurate. Without him the proprietor would have been sadly at sea, in his full knowledge of all connected with his department.

What was very remarkable in his case was that, in his full fidelity to his master, he did not compromise the respect and good will of his fellow servants. Among his own race he was the most universally popular servant on the whole estate, and had there been set up here a little Dominion of Dahomey, Uncle Philip would have been chosen king by universal acclaim. One can quite understand how such a servant should have been very much petted, but no indulgence seemed to spoil him. Do you see yonder house standing at the close of what the servants call Broadway, in that cluster of elm and maple trees? That is Uncle Philip's house. Let us enter it. In the first room you find shelves and hooks and racks around the walls. What do they mean? This is the old man's little storeroom. He was so absorbed in his devotion to his master's interests, so fully cut off thereby from the many little ways of making money for himself accorded the other servants, that he was allowed the privilege of his little store, where he kept a slender stock of staple goods —coffee, tea, sugar, cheese, cakes, peanuts, calico and home brewed beer (ginger and persimmon), with which he drove his little trades with his fellow servants; in lieu of money, often taking coon, rabbit, and squirrel skins as a circulating medium.

One would have been surprised to know how much money in the course of a year the old man took in. The writer when a boy would often exceed the allowance of pocket money from his mother. On the Southern plantation the rule was that the sons drew their pocket change from their mother until they were sent off to school, when the father became the son's banker. Often and ever, when out of money, the writer would borrow from Uncle Philip, who always insisted on a note given with a formal seal, at ninety or one hundred and twenty days after date, Remember, the old man did not know the boyish handwriting from Egyptian hieroglyphics. It was a matter of trust, pure and simple. Invariably, a few days before the note fell due the old man would approach the maker of the note, with the most respectful suggestion:

"Marse Jeems, you dun forget dat little paper of yourn, isn't you?"

Unless the writer wished his father to know of this transaction he had to stir around, get up the money and settle with his devoted old creditor, who insisted on payment of principal and interest, but who would immediately renew the loan if desired. It has always been a matter of mystery to me how he could figure up his interest so accurately, and yet I never knew him to make a mistake. This incident is here given that one may see the generous confidence and loving relation of the old plantation life between master and servant. If the writer meets with Mrs. Stowe in the next world he intends to acquaint her with much that did not appear in her ignorant compendia of anger, hatred and malice—that avant-coureur of the John Brown raid which was the skirmish line of 1861 and '65—that period of national dementia which, in its bitter and bloody antagonism to the law and order both of Holy Scripture and the Constitution, argued that prolongation of the godless French revolution. We shall now go on to the lake and acquaint the reader with the turpentine orchard and the distilleries of the spirits of turpentine and resin connected with this estate. Catherine Lake was the largest of a chain of seven or eight small lakes which we find in the midst of the twenty-two thousand acres of splendid pine trees embracing the turpentine orchards of this estate. This lake was about a half mile in length and from a quarter to three-eighths of a mile in breadth, in many places quite deep and in some places covered over with the pads of water lilies, in season very beautiful with their large white flowers. There was neither visible outlet nor inlet. It must have derived its bountiful and uniform supply of crystal water from hidden springs. It contained a large supply of small fish of the perch family, with a great many small turtles, or as the Negroes called them "tarrapins." In the winter season large droves of wild duck came from the rice fields and elsewhere to roost here. Come, get into this sail boat, and from yonder little island we will get a full view of the old planter's possessions on the south bank of this lake, and we will have a long, long talk about this branch of the plantation industries. Those large columns of black smoke you see issuing from those tall chimneys are from the two large distilleries you observe there, while that windmill drives the force which furnishes the large quantities of water required in the distillation of some hundreds of barrels of crude turpentine consumed daily. The process of distillation of spirits of turpentine for the world's markets is so like that of the distillation of whiskey and brandy that we do not regard it necessary to go into details. In that large cluster of houses nearby you will find the cooper shops and the large sheds for storing the barrel timber. Do you hear that merry ringing out of voices, in tuneful time to the coopers' adzes and drivers, as they force the hoops home on these barrels, used in the shipment of the white resin to New York and Boston? From each cooper were required forty-two barrels each week, and so easy was the task and so skilled were the best of them that they could readily enough make over and above their task from eight to ten barrels per week extra. Thus Dave and Sam and the other coopers had from eighty cents to a dollar in change to spend at Uncle Philip's store or to do what they pleased with on Saturday afternoon. Nearby is the glue house, where the casks used in the shipment of the spirits of turpentine were made good and tight; and there is the large and airy stabling for the numerous mules used in the heavy transportation of the crude turpentine to the distilleries, as well

84

as in hauling the manufactured article to the landing on the river some six miles away.

That comfortable looking home out there to the left is the summer house of the old planter, far away (some three miles) from the malaria that may be lurking around and the mosquitoes buzzing about the old mansion of the plantation proper, which we have already visited but only partly described.

An elaborate description of the coastal forest region of the South will not be here attempted. Suffice it to say that in the large area of the western part of the State of North Carolina, together with the Piedmont and coastal regions, are embraced more than three-fourths of the acreage of the whole State. The revenue in timber, lumber, and turpentine products has been variously estimated at from thirty-five to forty millions each year. Into these twenty thousand and more acres connected with this estate which we are describing let us at once enter with Uncle Philip, and we will listen while the writer is describing the mode by which these millions on millions of boxes are inserted into these large yellow pines, out of which the crude turpentine is taken to go into these distilleries for the world's market. The planter's New York market is largely regulated by the relation of supply and demand in the Liverpool and other European markets.

When you are about to take up a body of pine forests and reduce it to the culture of turpentine, what is the first thing you do?

"Listen, Uncle Philip, and see if I inform the reader correctly."

"Yes, suh, dat I will, Marse Jeems."

Well, the first thing you do is to burn over the wood, so as to throw them open by destroying all the undergrowth possible. Then the box cutters come, some twenty-five or thirty in number. In the late fall and all through the winter, when the sap is flowing more sluggishly, and when the cutting into the tree seems to injure them least, they are very busy. These splendid axemen come with their long, narrow-bladed, highly tempered axes, which are made by the blacksmith, Robert, on the plantation. They make seven or eight deep incisions in the shape of a crescent or new moon, about five inches above the ground, obliquely down into the tree. Then they hollow out behind these incisions towards the heart of the tree, and presently you will see how skillfully these axe men with their ringing strokes will complete one of these smoothly finished pockets or boxes as they are called. Then they corner them, as they call it; that is, they will smoothly notch these pockets at the corners, so as to cause the flow of the sap from the edges towards the center. How many of these will they insert into each tree? Some four or five. This depends on the size of the tree. You must be careful not to over box the tree—in failing to leave a space as broad or broader than a man's hand of untouched bark between the boxes—so that the sap will have plenty of room for free and rapid flow. What is the estimated capacity of the box? About a quart or a little over is the regulation size. How many of these in a day's task for each man A good axe-man will readily cut one hundred and twenty-five daily, will have finished his seven hundred and fifty by the middle of the afternoon on Friday, and have the remaining part of the week for himself. Thus your thirty hands will have finished in one week twenty-two thousand, five hundred? Yes. How many of these constitute a week's task for a good hand? Twelve thousand, five hundred are accounted a fair work for an average man to chip, or open the pores of each box, once each week. What do you mean by chipping? Each man is furnished with a tool called a round shave, which is of finely tempered steel, in the shape of a small knife, round and bent like your forefingers curved from the second joint, about an inch and a half in width, with a shank about seven inches in length to fit in a wooden handle. With this sharp instrument he scores horizontally just above the box or pocket and thus keeps the pores open and the sap running freely into the box. If the winter is an open or warm one the insertion of the box will have set the pine to bleeding so freely as to fill the box by the tenth of April. If so, another set of hands come with

86

their dippers and buckets, dip out the boxes and fill their buckets, which they empty into barrels dropped at convenient places here and there by Negro boys with their mule carts. These the carters bunch or gather together, so as to expedite the work of the wagons in hauling them to the distilleries, after they have been headed up by a cooper. Thus the work of chipping goes on without interruption each week, from about the fifteenth of April until the fifteenth of September — about five months — while the dippers go from one task or allotment of boxes to another, and so on regularly through the working season of five months. Each one of these dippers will dip out and fill four barrels daily, or twenty-four in a week. He will get through with his task on Friday; and on Saturday, by pushing on with his work, he will make from forty to sixty cents for himself. You will observe that by this plan of operation each crop will be reached by the dippers some four times each season, giving the planter from his orchard as many partial harvests each year, which to one understanding the judicious use of his money is a marked advantage over the cotton, sugar, tobacco or rice crops. When the nights begin to turn cool and the sap ceases to flow you will find that on the face of the box (the space between the chipping or the opening of the pores and the pocket or box) there will be a deposit of turpentine not unlike the whitest wax. This is the turpentine which has been hardened by the air. Into a box on four short legs at the base of the tree this deposit is scraped off and mixed with the contents of the pocket, and finds its way to the distilleries.

This closes the active operations of the year, which generally come about the first of November, when these laborers can be taken in to work on the plantation, opening ditches, clearing new ground or put to cutting other boxes in the virgin pines, if the planter wishes to extend his crop of boxes each year. The average chipper from his crop in five months will produce about five hundred barrels of about thirty-two gallons each, so that the sixty servants will in that time make about thirty thousand barrels, leaving some six months of the year to be employed, either in the extension of the turpentine orchard o.. in farm work, as the planter may elect. By joining these two industries, the orchards and the plantation, making the latter the full feeder of the former, you will readily understand how it is that the plantation can be kept, with its fine fencing, trim hedgerows, well worked roads, largely like a garden. How long will the average pine tree continue to yield its sap as above described? A crop of boxes will continue profitable for ten or twelve years. Is the tree worthless after that time? No. It yields fine wood, excellent lumber, but not the best—as largely drained of its essential oil in the turpentine extracted it cannot be as valuable for timber purposes as the untapped tree—yet in the markets of this country and Europe still valuable; notably so when not exposed to the weather but used for inside work, as in framing, flooring and ceiling. Then, too, many of these pines, after they have been cultivated for years, are cut out and from them are extracted the tar and pitch of the markets of the world. Do you regard these turpentine orchards, worked as indicated above, as profitable? One would think so if one would look at the account of the planter with his commission merchants in New York. You will see that his income is about sixty thousand dollars per annum, without reference to the yearly increased value of stock, lands and servants, which are by no means inconsiderable items or features of this steadily increasing wealth of the planter. Are the servants of the turpentine orchards generally healthy? There are no laborers in the world more so. The balsamic properties, which the pine tree is constantly distilling in the air, seem to counteract any poison from malaria. What water do they drink? Here and there are small but clear streams of running water all over these large tracts of pine-covered lands, and if the servant is out of condition you will see him take the joint of the ordinary reed, which he carries in his pocket for that purpose, kneel down at the base of a pine tree and slake his thirst from the rain water which has been caught in the box or pocket, impregnated as it is with the turpentine. This reaches and regulates his liver and keeps him healthy.

As compared with the other staples of the South, what do you regard as the most serious drawback or disadvantage of the planter's turpentine interests? The laborers, and notably so the chippers, are employed in large, wooded tracts of country, out of range of anything like close oversight and must be stimulated to their best work, as well by premiums for best crops as by so regulating their work that a portion of each week is their own to do as they please with. It is very different on the cotton, sugar, tobacco and rice plantations. The great disadvantage in the crop, however, is that the distilleries, the spirits of turpentine, the resin, and in fine the whole plant and its yields are so combustible that no insurance company, domestic or foreign, will insure the property. The only protection against fire that can be had is to police the premises as thoroughly as possible. How is this done? By placing here and there all over the orchards double log cabins for the families of some twenty or more white men. These people occupy these cabins free of rent, with as much land as they choose to cultivate, which rarely extends beyond a garden and truck patch, the men fishing and hunting by day and night, while the women hoe the little crops and raise poultry, the children gathering whortleberries and wild currants. These men are required to do three things; first, they are to guard the orchards from fire, and if a small fire occur, as it often does in the summer time by lightning striking and igniting a resinous pine tree, they and their families must extinguish it. If it gets beyond their control they are to blow horns, summon the neighboring tenants and, sending all around for help, fight the fire fiend until it is put out; secondly, they must once a week salt and care for the herd of cattle and drove of sheep belonging to the proprietor, carefully penning the sheep at night so as to protect them from the dogs, wildcats and bears, which are found in those large tracts of unbroken forests. Thirdly, they must look out for the planter's honey bees, and when the cold weather sets in they must take the honey and carry it into the mansion for the use of the planter's family. They are obliged, under contract, to turn out when summoned to work the roads of the estate. These tenants find a ready market for all the game, poultry and berries they will carry into the plantation. Sometimes they spend a whole lifetime in this dwarfed but important relation to the proprietor. They form a distinct element in the organism of this large landed estate. They never mingle with the more thrifty white people, while the Negroes on the estate look down upon them, calling them, most disdainfully, "poor white trash." Under the old regime this was the people who were unhappily affected by the plantation system, because they lived in the presence of and close contact with servile labor and lived and died with an emphatic protest against the decree, which forced them to work. From this class all through the coastal region, during the late Confederacy, sprang what was called the "buffalo," who cast in their lot with the federal troops as soon as any lodgment was made. They have not yet died out from among us, but still live, utterly contemned by the better class of whites and distrusted by Negroes.

"Well, Uncle Philip, how does this account agree with your view of it?"

"It's mi'ty nigh rite, Marse Jeems; youse made it mi'ty plain to dis old darky."

"Well, what does that heavy smoke mean over there, old man?"

"Why, suh, Harry, the distiller, is lettin' off his heavy charge of rosun and dat is de smoke yo' see, suh. Marse Jeems, it's about twelve o'clock, suh, and I must be goin.'"

So to the mainland we go, and when about half way, where the water is quite deep, and we see the tall bodies of the large pines standing all around the rim of the lake, not unlike the palisades on the Hudson River, Uncle Philip takes a long tin bugle and giving a full blast upon it wakes up the echoes far and near, which come back to us in wave sounds very deep and at times very sweet. Peaching the shore, the writer goes around to a

90

secluded cove and, in the crystal waters of the lake, enjoys a delightful bath, with a good, long swim, after an old-fashioned dive from the spring board with which this deep pool is furnished. After the hath he is joined by the old planter at lunch, where some of the lake fish are discussed, together with a cup of Maria's best coffee and the eggs, fried to a turn on both sides, followed by a plate of wild, currants and cream. Just such a lunch for all the world as would make a Southern man's mouth water, even if he were at Harvey's in Washington or at Delmonico's in New York.

CHAPTER IX.

Interchanges of courtesies quite common among the plantations before the war.

AT LUNCH it is agreed upon that we go some four of five miles south of the lake, for the double purpose of inspecting a road which is being opened in that part of the orchard and of salting the sheep and cattle. When he is mounted you will be struck with some features of the planter's outfit. You observe what a fine rider he is, as like a centaur he sits that beautiful horse of his, gliding along in that perfection of gaits, the fox trot of the Southern saddle horse, so easy, so undulating as scarcely to move the dear old gentleman in his firm seat. What is that tied so securely to the back of his saddle? That is a wallet of stout, homespun cloth, in one section of which, were you to inspect it, you would find a number of ready-made wooden wedges of different sizes, with which to wedge up the gates of the plantation if one of them should be found not to swing easily on its hinges, while in another department you would find strips of leather in the shape of both throat-latches for the bridle and ham-strings as well, with a number of "nubbins" or small ears of corn for any pig or heifer which he may meet with in his ride. What is that buckled, in its leather case, so securely to the bow of his saddle? That is his keen-edged hatchet, which, with splendid silver-mounted, double-barreled shotgun, constitutes his outfit. Do you observe how large and deep are the skirts of his beautiful Nashville saddle? Why are they so large? To protect his limbs from the sweat of his horse. Do you observe that beautiful broad-brimmed Guayaquil (a place-name on Ecuador where this type hat was made) straw hat he is wearing and how nicely gloved he is, while you must he struck with the highly polished steel spurs he is wearing? How sharp the rowels are. Those spurs are polished every morning by his body servant, "Buck," as regularly as are his boots. Thus mounted the writer thinks that not even General Joe Johnston or Wade Hampton or Ashby himself were finer riders. As he calls out to Buck to follow on with his sack, partially filled with salt, tied behind him on his mule, we ride along together, talking of crops, the weather and politics with that absence of reserve and that peculiarly tender abandon characterizing the relation of the old Southern planter and his children, for there was no aloofness of bearing here. Though the years have run into decades since that bright portion of his life, and the blood runs rather sluggishly in his old veins, yet, with blessed retrospect, the pulses of life quicken and he finds himself calling out to himself, "Would I were a boy again."

What large spaces are those on the right and left of the road leading away to the southwest? They are two of the small prairies or meadows, of seventy-five or a hundred acres each, with which these turpentine orchards abound, in many cases without a single tree of any size upon them. Their conformation is that of a large, shallow saucer, thickly set with a variety of wild grasses and embellished by myriads of lovely wild flowers, among which are the scarlet Indian pink and the dwarfed honeysuckle, while the air is redolent with the perfume of the wild vanilla, giving out its odor, as its leaves are bruised by the feet of the cattle and the sheep grazing out there as you see. How fine is the effect of these beautiful meadows, hedged around by those tall, stately, forest sentinels, those magnificent yellow pines of dear old Southland, by all odds the most useful of all the trees in the American forests! On all these meadows, many in number, on this estate, you might readily graze two or three thousand cattle; thus it is, with the fine winter pasturage of the salt marshes, there is not a month in the year in which the old planter could not have from his own shambles fine beef and mutton. These wild grasses here are often very tall and luxuriant, coming up in height to your feet in the stirrup, as one rides along to yonder ridge where the salt is given the cattle in long wooden troughs, around which in droves

94

they have already gathered in eager expectancy, for they have already sniffed the salt in Buck's big bag behind him on the mule, as salt is indeed the savor of life.

We had already reached the center of the larger meadow on the left when the conversation ceased, as is often the case when one is in sweet communion with nature, as here in one of her loveliest moods—the meadowlands crowned with their rich product of natural grasses, the honey bee busy in gathering her nectared sweets from the myriads of wild flowers blooming in such rich profusion all around, the only sound heard the lowing of the kine[10] and the plaintive bleating of the sheep—in Indian file we were making our way towards the salting ground, with the old planter in the lead and Buck bringing up the rear, when, as sudden as a bolt from heaven and as quick as thought, there rang out on the air, "Bang! bang!" What does it mean? We had come upon two fine deer. Approaching them to the leeward they could not smell us, the footfall of our horses' feet being muffled by the lush grass they could not hear us, while their cover was so deep they could not see us, and we had come bluff up on two old bucks, when, with his fine aim and long ranged gun, the planter had covered them both before they could get out of range. Startled as they sprang up, they had fled in opposite directions but all to no purpose, for before they had reached the cover of the pine forests down they both went, when my father turned and called out in strong tones, "Got them both, son, by George!"

And so he had, for in less time than is required to tell of it the sharp blade of the pocket knife had passed over the jugular of both, and Buck's face was radiant with delight as he called out:

"Shure as yo' is born, Marse Jeems, ole marster is de bes' shot in Norf Ca'liny."

---

[10] Middle English, kyn, Old English, cȳna, genitive plural of cū or cow.

The cattle were soon salted, and the smaller of the two bucks was secured behind the saddle of the planter without any difficulty. When it came to tying the other buck on the Negro's mule we had no easy task, for, whether or not it comes from close association with each other, both Negroes and mules are afraid of the dead. Finally we succeeded after much coaxing and, the last resort in such cases, blindfolding the mule. All the way home Buck was kept in a state of fear lest the mule should "roach"' his back, which is the asinine mode of putting his muscles in such fearful battery as would have landed with .fearful force Buck, saddle, deer and all promiscuously on the breast of mother earth. Thus laden with fine venison our gait was indeed a slow one. However, we soon struck the main road about a mile from the homestead, where we overtook a long line of wagons heavily laden with lumber from the planter's saw mill at the lake. These wagons en route from the landing, where they had carried their heavy freightage of spirits of turpentine and resin, had stopped at the distilleries and were on their way home with lumber for the uses of the plantation. Early next morning Buck, on mule back, was dispatched with a large old-fashioned basket (woven on the plantation of the pliant splits of white oak) in which choice roasts and steaks of venison were carried to the planters' wives of the neighboring estates, with a kind note from him whose fine marksmanship we have witnessed.

These interchanges of such courtesies were quite common among the plantations before the war. Dwelling among their own people, remote from the towns, the old planter and his family were largely dependent for society upon their neighbors; and in those blessed Arcadian days, before prurient materialism had laid such baneful hold upon our population, social life at the South had taken on such fine forms as to make it the admiration of all who came in contact with it. It was then that citizenship at the South rose to its high water mark, possessing those who wore it with such social charms and buttressed on such high integrity, long before the dark days of "credit mobilier,"[11] as to make it very influential all over the land. But these days have passed away. "Times change and we change with them," said the old pagan. The era of cui bono philosophy, with its cognate of "Honesty is the best policy," is upon us now, wrapping around our lares and penates its certificates of stocks in such transforming and deforming manner and results, as well-nigh to hide them out of view. It was during these better days of the republic that from the South were furnished to the nation such statesmen as King of Alabama, Badger of North Carolina, Reeves of Virginia, Reverdy Johnson of Maryland, Crittenden and Breckenridge of Kentucky, and a host of others so noted for high courage and deep insight into the genius of republican institution—allied with such fine forms of statesmanship and such incorruptible integrity—as to constitute them and others like them the very guardians of the country.

We have spoken of the hospitality of the South. Let us close this chapter by an incident, which will serve the purpose of its illustration, bringing out some of the customs of the planter's family, while shedding some light upon the characteristics of the servants who dwelt at that time so happily in their freedom from care and responsibility, with their old master, under the vine and fig tree of his ample and loving provision. Under a charter from one of the Charleses there came from old England before the Revolution of the American colonies a large band of Scotch people, who settled in the upper Cape Fear section of North Carolina. Their descendants are still there and embrace among

---

[11] Crédit Mobilier was part of a complex arrangement whereby a few men contracted with themselves or assignees for the construction of the railroad. Along with certain trustees, the manipulators reaped enormous profits but impoverished the railroad in the process. The Crédit Mobilier scandal of 1872-1873 damaged the careers of several Gilded Age politicians. Major stockholders in the Union Pacific Railroad formed a company, the Crédit Mobilier of America, and gave it contracts to build the railroad. They sold or gave shares in this construction to influential congressmen.

97

their unnumbered "Macs" some of the very best citizens of the old State. Of course, in coming from Scotland they brought with them that national fondness for letters and those peculiar religious dogmas that constituted them old-fashioned Presbyterians, pure and simple. Holding their religious faith with the tenacity of Moslems they, by well-directed missionary work, sought to introduce it into other parts of the State. Informed at home by the young and well educated Scotchmen, who had gone down as teachers in the families of the planters in the tidewater country, both of the wealth there abounding and of the absence of any and all allegiance to the Westminster catechism, with their characteristic zeal they sent their missionaries down there to lengthen the cords and strengthen the stakes of Zion in this neglected part of the State. In the old county of Onslow, in which the scene of this incident is laid, there was not a single organized congregation of Presbyterians. Of course a missionary was sent here, a noble representative of his high and holy faith he was, combining great pastoral activity with such powers as a preacher and allied with such purity and simplicity of life, as enabled him in his marked popularity and extended usefulness to preach the word of God to crowded congregations. He was very popular, and nowhere more so than at the home of the writer's father, where he was always a most welcome guest. On one of his many visits to the old home, after family worship one night, he was shown to his chamber by Handy, the dining room servant, who, with a pair of slippers under his arm and the old-fashioned candlestick with spermaceti candle in it in the other hand, lighted the holy man of God up to the prophet's chamber. After entering the room Handy waited some little time for the divine to draw off his boots, that he might take them downstairs and polish them for the next day's use. There stood the Negro waiting for the boots. The clergyman, utterly ignoring the presence of the boy, in that absent mindedness often found in those whose sweetest pleasure is in close communion with dead men in their books, proceeded to pour out a little water in a goblet; then, standing before the

98

mirror, with great dexterity, he unshipped an eye and placed it in the goblet. This unfamiliar, uncanny scene shook the nerves of the Negro very severely; yet, thoroughly trained to obedience, he held his ground. But when, standing before the looking-glass, the Scotch parson proceeded to take out a set of false teeth, Handy could stand the performance no longer. Dashing down the slippers, and waiting no longer for the boots nor for anything else, he rushed down the stairway and never stopped until he landed in the kitchen, where, out of breath from the rapid gait whereby he emphasized his fearful fright, he called out to the old cook as test he could write his short breathing, "A'nt Patty, flat, dat, dat dar preecherman upstairs farely takin' hisself all to pieces." Said the old cook, "You'd bettah go back and git him boots, yuh fool negur." "No, ma'm, I wouldn't go up dem sta'rs to-nite fur his boots full ob money." Nor did he go until the daylight of the next morning gave him the full assurance that there were no ghosts or hobgoblins, in the form of a preacher man, to do him harm.

Ah, these blessed old plantation servants, with all their fine forms of beautiful devotion to duty, how very superstitious they were; and yet not at all more so than the corresponding class in the older civilizations of Europe. After all is not human happiness hindered rather than promoted by that excess of one-sided education which in unfettering the intellect so enchains the heart and its sweet affections as to eliminate from the problem of human life those factors of reverence and docility which, in the blind worship of cold Egoism, is wrecking the faith of the world?

Typical slave quarters. This picture is from the files of the Library of Congress and is in the public domain because of its age.

99

CHAPTER X.

A description of a day in the life of a slave on a North Carolina plantation, as recalled by the author.

SO MUCH is there to be said of the old plantation life to those who discover any interest in the manners, customs and other formative influences of the ante-bellum Southland, that we may have tarried too long in the description of the turpentine orchards. Yet this can scarcely be so to those who are both proud of and interested in their ancestors. French novels may come in by the score (bringing in such brain products as those of Zola, and others of his stamp), and by their prurient realism may impair the purity of our lighter literature. Clubs may be organized for the discussion of such authors as Mrs. Humphrey Ward and others of her stamp, but the healthy Anglo-Saxon mind is so strongly attached to the masters of the British classics that we may rest secure in the possession of the writings of Thackeray, Scott, Bulwer (in his better days and purer works) and the incomparable Dickens, in their fine influence over our children. In America it will be a long, long time before our own Fennimore Cooper, delighting, in his "Leather Stocking Tales," to tell us of the Indian summer, that honeymoon of the year, in which one loves to recall the names of those who made nature a great white throne where men might kneel or dream or worship) will have failed to influence the youth of our land. And this is so, not because he was a delineator of nature, so much as because he keeps us in loving touch with the past and its blessed traditions and influences, so potent in the coinage of a splendid type of genuine manhood. We believe that, in keeping our children well informed of their ancestral virtues we shall furnish them with the most healthy corrective of much, in the last quarter of the nineteenth century's electric social condition, which to the mind furnished and strengthened by the philosophy of history must present itself as most enervating and harmful in many ways. Therefore it is that this book is written; that the effort is made to preserve pure and inviolate the annals of the Southern people, at such a time as they were fortunately possessed of a record of their own; when in their own pure homogeneity they challenged the admiration of all who knew them in their sunlit God-kept homes. We have, in part, described the old plantation and its many servants, telling how they lived—their homes, their rations of good, healthy food and the warm clothing they wore—we have seen in all this much to confirm the opinion that no peasantry in the world were ever more comfortably provided for than they were when they had humane masters. Humane the great majority of the old plantation masters were, notwithstanding the sickly creation of Mrs. Stowe's distempered fancies. These people on these estates were the property of the planter, with full warranty of Holy Scripture for their possession, if the unanswered letters of the late Bishop Hopkins of Vermont to the late Bishop Potter of Pennsylvania prove anything. The Supreme Court of the United States so adjudged, until the Constitution was overridden in the triumph of sectionalism, with its irrepressible conflict of "higher law" with the basic principles of the Federal Constitution. Beside all this (and no man has ever answered the argument of the Bishop of Vermont, that remarkable prelate, who never lived a day among or drew a dollar from the Southern people) these planters were amenable to the laws of self-interest and common sense, which alike forbade the abuse and ultimate destruction of their own property. Neither Jay Gould nor Mr. Bonner thus treated their fast trotters. On the contrary they nourished them with the tenderness given their own children.

Something must now be said of the hours of plantation work. Uncle Ben brought a long blast on his horn from the window of his own room after the day had broken. This was the signal for the three men servants to come down from their quarters and feed all the animals, horses, mules and oxen, to be employed that day on plantation work. After which these same men went to the well near the gin house and filled the several large casks mounted on wheels with healthful water, so that when the assembly bell rang at Uncle Jim's cabin about sunrise the plowmen might take this potable water across the creek for the wants of the day. Meantime all had breakfasted. At sunrise the assembly bell rang out long and loud; then the servants, under the direction of the foremen, who had received their orders the night before from the planter in his office at the mansion, filed out in order and went their way to the day's work; the forty plowmen following their leader, Uncle Suwarro, and the larger number of hoe men and women, boys and girls, were led by their foreman, Uncle Jim. "Gee! Whoa! Back!" What does that mean? Uncle Harry and the other ox cart drivers are yoking up their oxen, and presently you could see the five or six ox teams filing out of the big gate as up the cedar avenue they went. Faithful old Harry had his orders for the day's work, in hauling rails for a line of new fence, or to repair an old line, or in large loads of marl or other plantation work. By this time Uncle Jack, with five other drivers of the six mule teams, was cracking his long wagon whip as with one line over his fine leader he drove out of the gate en route to the lake and the work in the orchards.

pleasure horses, knowing which were to be in use this morning, while Aunt Abby and Emeline were to be seen making their way up the hill with buckets of foaming milk to the dairy. The bellows in the blacksmith shop began to puff and blow as Robert and Washington ranged themselves for the day's work, and the hammers and the saws in the carpenter shop told that George, Virgil and Jim were at work. Thus was it that by the time the breakfast bell at the great house had rung this hive of industry was buzzing, each and all at their own work. No unnecessary noise, no confusion, but all in the quiet order with which each had gone to his own work, showing what the

103

discipline of a superior mind over servants could and did accomplish.

Born in Dublin Ireland, John Henry Hopkins (1792 –1868) was the first bishop of the Episcopal Diocese of Vermont. In 1861, he published a pamphlet entitled "A Scriptural, Ecclesiastical, and Historical View of Slavery." This image is in the public domain because its copyright has expired.

Cicero and Henry were busy now in feeding, grooming and watering the various

After breakfast, if you would like to do so, we will ride out and see what these servants are all about. How shall we go? Shall we ride or drive? The large plantation is so laid out with fine wagon roads that we can go in the light carriage through all the fields. Well, then, we'll drive. So after breakfast off we went, with Cicero driving a pair of light horses to a wagon purchased in Wilmington, Delaware, and known as the "jump-seat surrey"— that is, a vehicle so finished that you could unfold the seats and carry four persons, while from its light structure it was intended ordinarily for two people. Those are two fine horses, and admirably matched they seem to be, but of small size. Tell me something about them. These horses are a cross between the wild ponies, found in large numbers on the long, narrow islands flanking the coast of North Carolina, and that large fine stallion, "Crackaway," you see the groom leading back to his stable after having given him water. This cross makes a very serviceable animal for light use, taking their high mettle from the thoroughbred sire and the tough endurance from the wild dam. You see they do not lack speed (let them go, Cicero), and off we go at a rapid rate up the broad, smooth road until we reach the barnyard on the opposite side of the creek, about three-fourths of a mile away, when we get out of the carriage, and attention is drawn to the various appointments for the distinctive breeding of the several kinds of hogs. We never saw finer specimens of the Berkshire, with his small, pointed ears, broad shoulders, short, thick-set head, small, tapering legs, and prevalent white and

104

black spots about the size of the palm of your hand. This fine hog, thoroughly bred and carefully fatted, accounts for the superiority of the planter's fine old hams. Over there in those breeding pens you observe the old planter has his Essex, Chester whites and Jersey Reds, but none so fine as the Berkshire; while, more for the sake of variety than for intrinsic value, he keeps a few of the little Guineas, which to the hog family is largely what the bantam is to the ordinary breed of fowls, trim and trig, but never large. You will quite understand the size and fine quality of those fine oxen you saw this morning if you will go with me over to those stock lots and look at that fine Durham bull. Did you ever see a nobler specimen? He was shipped from the valley of the Connecticut River when a calf and is now fully grown, about seven years of age. In that other lot nearby is another fine animal of the Devon or Shorthorn breed. He was presented to the old planter when a calf by his very dear friend, the Honorable William S. Ashe, M.C., and sent from one of the largest stock farms in Maryland. Thus you see how particular and fortunate in the selection of his stock the proprietor of this estate has been. But the morning is wearing away and we have only time just now to take a look at those brood mares and the colts by their sides in that large pasture lot on the opposite side of the road. Do you observe how flat their legs are, what small, pointed ears they have, how sharp in their withers, how short and close their coupling, what large, full nostrils, and how red the lining is, and, with all these points of a thoroughbred, what long and graceful necks they have, with their thin manes, small pastern joints and very small fetlocks? Again, you see that sorrel is the prevailing color, and that while evidently they are all of them high spirited, yet how docile they are and how they love to be petted, as they eat these lumps of sugar from the writer's hand. These seven colts are the foals of the celebrated Trustee, the sire of Fashion, the empress of the American turf. They are the pride of the planter's heart, among all his possessions of blooded animals, and justly so, for they look already,

"As though the speed of thought were in their limbs."

In this large pasture field, extending on both sides of the creek, with great boulders of detached limestone rock, you observe how rough and broken the land is? Why is this? Not accidentally, but designedly; because the proprietor was taught by a very successful stock raiser in Kentucky always to select rough, hilly ground for his mares and colts, in order that the latter, in growing up, may have the finer development of muscle. This is so, doubtless, on the same principle, that the Scotch highlander is far better developed physically in his rough mountain home than is the Hollander in his flat country along the Zuyder Zee. Well, here we are at the carriage again. Let us drive on. What are all those people doing over there among those vines? They are giving the large crop of sweet potatoes their last working, before they are laid by. You observe they are hilling them up, after they have cut off many of the vines to the length of eight or ten feet. The vines thus cut off they will place in those open furrows on the top of those long ridges you see over there, and by putting a hoe-full of earth eighteen or twenty inches apart these vines will take root and make the crop of seed potatoes for another year—"slips" as they are called, not growing much larger, if any, than a man's thumb, but plenty large. What varieties of the potato are planted here? Generally the yam for the table and the Spanish for stock purposes, as the former abound in saccharine matter, while the latter is far more prolific in its yield. Why is the potato planted in long, narrow strips, not wider than seventy-five or an hundred yards? In order the more readily to fence them off in small lots when feeding them to the fattening hogs in the early fall of the year. You observe what system, what method, with their rationale, obtain on this plantation in its various crops. You see we have at length reached Uncle Suwarro, with his large force of plowmen. Here they come through the beautiful green corn, just now coming into what they call the bush, before it begins to shoot and tassel; that is, before it begins to show the outline of the ear beginning to form or to blossom

106

out with its pollen, with which to fructify the ear of corn. Let us see what they are doing? You observe here in the upland, in rows more than a half mile long, in some of the fields the corn crop is planted with its stalks in hills four and a half feet apart each way. The old foreman, in his shirt sleeves and broad brimmed straw hat, woven by his wife or daughter out of the oat straw of the plantation, is abreast of nineteen others, throwing the earth with their plows well up to the corn, leaving a mellow bed into which the vigorous plant shoots its lateral roots, as well for nourishment as to enable the stalks to withstand the autumnal gales, which are sure to come about the equinox and which would otherwise lay the crop flat on the ground, thus causing much of the corn to be lost. Following these plowmen, what are those twenty half grown boys and girls doing? They are planting the black-eyed pea crop, which you will see later on, is a very important one. Do you observe that large gourd, looking like a small basket, which each one of these young Negroes is carrying on his left side, supported by a leather strap across the right shoulder? In these are carried the seed peas, and as they pass a hill of corn you observe that with a quick and a regular motion of the right hand holding a charger (made out of a bit of gourd neck with a short handle) they drop from twelve to fourteen of these peas in the furrow just opened and directly opposite the hill of corn. The twenty plowmen following after, split out the middles of these rows, covering the peas and still hilling up the corn. Now when this field of corn is cross plowed and treated in exactly the same way, the result will be that the hill of corn, generally of two stalks will be the center of a quadrangle, with a hill of peas at each one of the four angles. You will quite understand the proprietor of this estate, when, in speaking of the value of his pea crop, he says, that it more than pays all of its own expense and that of making the large corn crops. To what use is the crop of peas put? First, when the crop is ripe they are gathered in large hamper baskets and carefully stored away, and in the winter and early spring they are fed in large quantities to the sheep and milch cows, for they are both grain and forage. Many of th" finest are carefully put away for the seed of the ensuing year. In the richest portions of the plantation many are cut down with scythes and dried and stacked for the oxen and mules. Thus when all this has been done and the corn has been gathered out of these fields, the large number of hogs, upon which the planter is dependent for the meat rations of his people, are turned in to glean these fields of the shattered or un-gathered corn by day and are turned in on the sweet potatoes by night. In addition to this, this practical old planter plants in each field of corn some five or six acres of peanuts, or ground peas for his hogs. These nuts are full of oil and they serve to put the oncoming animals of the planter's shambles in the finest possible condition for the table. You can quite understand the value of the pea crop, more valuable by far than either the crimson or white clover, with just this one disadvantage, that it is an annual and must be regularly renewed, while the clover is a perennial plant. Well, we have reached the point at the nick of time. It is just twelve o'clock and in a minute or so, as soon as he reaches the end of his row, you will hear the long-drawn, mellow notes of the dinner horn, as Uncle Suwarro blows it long and loud, calling his band of sixty laborers, with their animals, from labor to refreshment. My sakes! What unearthly racket is that we hear? It is indeed a hybrid of sound between a trombone and a fog horn! Whence does it come? It's the braying of forty mules, as they signal their joy on hearing the well-known call to dinner. No more work for them now. Not another row will they plow until they have been taken out of harness, taken to the nearest feeding station and given water and feed. Meantime let us see what these Negroes, these "slaves" of the old plantation, are to have from the baskets for their midday meal. The noon hour in the summer time ordinarily lasts from twelve o'clock to two P.M., So that both servants and animals may have ample time for food and refreshment. The animals have all been fed, and here and there, under the grateful shade of the splendid old black walnut and hickory trees, small fires have been kindled. Soon "the air is laden with the appetizing odors of the large strips or slices of fat mess pork, which to the average Negro is far more welcome than either beefsteak or mutton chops. This cooking process of theirs furnishes in their frying pan a plentiful supply of savory gravy, which they thin down with water. Into this they put their corn meal, which they stir until fully cooked and allowed to brown. Sometimes they will chop up the young onions, leaves, bulb and all, into this "cush," as they call it. In place of the onions they sometimes introduce the watercress from the bank of the creek. This, with their meat and bread and such vegetables as their gardens afford, gives them an abundant and nourishing meal. After this they sometimes indulge their fondness for sweets from the black bottle of molasses or sorghum, an abundance of which is produced on the plantation. Then to both men and women come the indispensable pipe and tobacco, or to the men the quid or "chaw" of this wonderful weed, all home grown in full abundance. After this they will either rest under the trees or join in pitching quoits, which they call "quakes," or in playing "five corns." This latter game with them takes the place of the old Roman game of dice. They take five grains of corn, large and plump, hollow out the heart or kernel, and, with their hands for a dice box, seek to throw all five of the grains of corn in such dexterous way as to bring down on the ground with all the hearts uppermost; the party first scoring twenty-five points wins the game, as they throw alternately. Sometimes they will play the game of "mumble peg," or they will engage in a game of ball, in the throwing or batting of which they discover as much dexterity in some cases as can be found on the modern baseball ground. Sometimes the older women can be seen busy with their plain simple sewing or knitting; while the men are engaged in putting a bottom in a chair, employing either corn shucks, the stems of the wild flag or splits of white oak. Many of them are busy in making baskets, some of large size, used in gathering the cotton crop and for various other plantation purposes, and others

109

smaller and of more delicate texture, for key baskets or for gathering up the eggs from the poultry yard. In all of these little industries they may not show the skill of the Indians in their work sold to tourists at Niagara Falls, but they certainly do display no little dexterity. The most industrious among them send their wares to New Berne or Wilmington, by the servants who drive the market wagons, and thus in the course of the year they gather in quite a nice little sum of money. It must not be forgotten, in estimating the slender income of these simple-hearted, unconventional servants of the old plantation, that they pay no rent, settle no doctor's bills, have naught to do with either grocer or butcher, and are free from the rapacity of the modern undertaker. In many respects the advantages of the servants on this plantation over those white slaves employed in the factories of both Old and New England was very marked, and in no respect more emphatically so than in the perfect exemption of the old plantation servant from the carking care and killing responsibility of the white laborers, telling so fearfully in their heavy bills of mortality and the very slow ratio of increase. So say statistics. At two o'clock the old foreman calls everybody from refreshment to labor and off they go to their afternoon work, until such time as will allow them to get to the quarter before the night sets in, allowing plenty of margin for the careful currying and grooming of their horses and mules. With the old planter it was a faithfully observed plantation maxim that the free and regular use of the currycomb and brush on all his animals, winter and summer, was more than equal to a fourth meal in keeping them up to a high standard of usefulness.

CHAPTER XI.

Going fishing with the Negroes on the plantation.

THE REGULAR plowmen did not feed their animals either at night or in the morning. This was done by a detail of three servants, made each week by Uncle Ben, and under his watchful eye the stock were all well cared for. The work on the plantation varied with the season, both as to its character and activity. While the crops of tobacco, rice, sorghum, cotton, wheat, oats, rye and corn were to be planted, cultivated or harvested, in every department of the plantation work there was marked activity. When the harvests were over there was a decided relaxation of energy, and yet the more sheltered and less exacting industries of the winter went on regularly and systematically. As has already been stated, there was no work for the master done on the plantation (except in harvest seasons) after twelve o'clock (noon) on Saturdays. My father was fully convinced that in this judicious mode of encouraging his servants in this half-holiday each week, in all departments of the large and complicated industries of the plantation, he accomplished far more in five and a half days of labor than he could have done by the steady grind, grind of six unbroken days of toil. With him it was not only "that a merciful man is merciful to his beast," but that a wise and thrifty master was kind to and considerate of his servants. To put it on the low plane of economics, leaving humanity and philanthropy out of view, it paid well to feed well, to house comfortably and to work judiciously the race which Anglo-Saxon civilization was gradually lifting up from the paganism in which English, New England and Spanish ship owners found it on the coast of Africa. The writer is about to close this chapter upon the various employments of the servants on the plantation and would gladly introduce an incident of his own life connected with that of dear old Uncle

Jim, the foreman, as we have seen, of the force of hoe-men on the estate.

Long, long years ago, in the late forties, when the writer was a mere slip of a boy, he obtained permission from his mother, as he often did, to go fishing with Uncle Jim, taking with him his boy, Cain, as was his habit. In this portion of the South there was an unwritten law by which the boy child born on the plantation nearest the birthday of the young master was his, and as the two came along together through childhood, boyhood, and all along through manhood, they were closely associated, having taken their first lessons together in riding, swimming, fishing, boat sailing, and in the various employments of outdoor life. Thus they were inseparable, while there was a blending of influences each upon the other, coming from that irresistible law of assimilation from close association; the Caucasian, from the very law of nature because the stronger of the two civilizations, exercising the stronger and more formative influence and shaping and molding the weaker. It was said on the plantation that Cain walked and talked like "Marse Jeems." Of this much there was no doubt, on Sundays and other holidays the young African dressed like the young master, for had they not the same tailor? Yes, except that Cain's use of the clothing was second-hand, and yet they fitted him so nicely when he was fully dressed up he would sing out most enjoyably, with his fine, rich voice:

"When I go out to lemonade
A dress so fine and gay
I'm "bleeged' (obliged) to take my dog along
To keep the gals away."

And surely at such times, in his even-tenored, uneventful life, Cain was the happier of the two; for while he, had not "a million a minute and expenses paid," he had all of Tits expenses paid, and cared nothing because he knew nothing of the misery of millionarism. Vanderbilt may have had a more showy and expensive body servant, but never one more faithful, more affectionate and, in simple role of duty, more efficient than this young African. Well, the time has come for this Saturday afternoon fishing excursion and off we go, with Uncle Jim carrying his own fishing rod and Cain taking his own and that of the young master, who comes along with his light double-barreled shotgun, so as to be ready for any squirrel, mink or otter which may be found. Cain gives a keen whistle for "Nat," the water spaniel, and soon we are down at the river bank, with plenty of angle or fish worms in small gourds around the two servants' necks, well stoppered with bits of corncob in lieu of corks. Uncle Jim said that the moon was right and that the wind was blowing from the right quarter for good luck. The old fellow cautions us to be very quiet, "as the fish doan' want no movin' about dem when dey is a-takin' dar meals." So we were as quiet as mice and the hooks were well baited with angle worms, the old man spitting on his bait for luck before he noiselessly dropped his hook in the water at the roots of a large cypress tree, among some chunks of wood held there by the eddy in the bend of the river. Well, we had not fished long before a peculiar grunt of satisfaction was heard and the whirring noise of a fishing line in the water, with the cork out of sight, told its tale of fine game fish at hand. It was a scene for a painter, that of Uncle Jim as, with every feature of his fine old ebon face keenly alert, he saw his tackle, rod and line, all standing the strain given them by a three-pound beauty of a fresh water trout. No amateur on Lake George, in New York State, nor even that ex-President of the United States, Cleveland, so far famed or rather notorious, for antagonizing the simplicity and honesty of the band of Galilean fishermen, ever landed his game with more ease, grace or joy than did this simple-hearted, born sportsman.

"Marse Jeems, wa'n't dat splendid? Be mi'ty still. His mate is dun gone in dar, and I'se bound to ketch him. Cain, yuh' fool negur, yuh, why doan' yuh keep less noise?

113

Quiet was restored and the fishing resumed. After a few moments the writer's cork was carried with great rapidity out of sight and he was drawing away on his rod with no little energy, while his line was cutting the water with a swishing sound, when the old fisherman called out:

"Gib 'im line, Marse Jeems, gib 'im line; doan' pull 'im so hard, suh. You'll broke your line, shuah (sure) as yuh is bo'n." (born)

The writer obeyed the instructions of the old fisherman, who, to his great relief, gently took the rod out of his hand and presently landed a very large eel. Whereupon he called out:

"Run here, Cain; run here, Cain; run here quick; fetch a stick and hit 'im hard as ever yuh can; not on de haid, (head) dat ain't any way to kill 'im. Hit 'im on de tail, hit 'im on de tail, you fool negur yuh, as hard as yuh kin."

After repeated blows on the eel's tail, which I shall always think was his head, Cain replied:

"He dun dead now, Uncle Jim," whereupon the old man took out his pocketknife and soon cut out the hook which the eel had voraciously swallowed with the bait.

Very soon thereafter the faithful old darky pulled up his line and moved off to other fishing grounds, saying half aloud and to himself:

"'Tain't no use a-fishin' heah no mo', Marse Jeems. Luck is all gone. Let's move down de ribber, for when yuh ketch one ob dese damn eels, Marse Jeems, he bustes up yer luck."

We went on down the river to other fishing grounds, and as we were moving along old Jim's conscience began to upbraid him for swearing in my presence, when in serio-comic tone of voice he inquired if I thought "cussin' dat eel was de same as swearin'."

By the time we reached the next place where we were to try our luck the old man's mind was fully at rest on the point he had raised and we betook ourselves to our sport with such success that long before the sun had set we had a very fine string of fish, the old man catching by far the greater quantity, while Cain and I

114

helped to swell the number of small fry. About this time we heard the ringing report of a rifle and soon Uncle Amos, the old sportsman, came in sight with quite a large number of squirrels and a brace or two of summer ducks, his contribution to the planter's table. It was not long after this, as we were making our way back home and had reached the gate of the back yard, when Uncle Jim asked me to get my mother's permission to let me come around next morning and see just how nice the fish were when Aunt Patty cooked them in her way. My mother consented, so, as I had done often before, next morning about eight o'clock I made my way to the old man's cabin, and such a breakfast as I did eat. His good old wife had gotten down her best "chaney," white with blue rimming, while the cloth on the table was as white as snow, and the floor spotlessly neat with its heavy sprinkling of white sand.

"Breakfas' is ready, Marse Jeems; set up, suh, and jus' help yo'self."

And this I did most certainly—to fish that were cooked to a turn, gashed and well sprinkled with corn meal and fried in the gravy of the mess pork, while the eggs were brown on both sides and such corn bread as you never see in these days, with excellent coffee, as clear as amber, settled with the shells of the eggs. When ample justice had been done this excellent meal I arose to go, for I knew that neither of these faithful souls would touch a morsel as long as I was in the house. Just as I was about to say "Good morning" to them the old man said:

"Marse Jeems, is yo' in mi'ty big hurry dis mornin'?"

I told him no.

"Jus' wait a minute, pleas', suh."

Whereupon the old man went into the bedroom and, unlocking his wooden "chist," which served the purpose of a trunk, he took out something which he brought into the front room. I saw it was a small gourd and nearly filled with salt. He turned to me and, in a very solemn voice said:

"Marse Jeems, dis ole negur is gittin' powerful' ole an' I jes' want to ax one little faber ob yuh."

"Very well, Uncle Jim, what is it? I'll do it if I can," I said.

This seemed to give him no little relief. With strengthened voice he said:

"In dis heah gode, Marse Jeems, is dis heah piece of my ear, dat yo' doan' see up heah," pointing to the missing part of his right ear. "You see, suh, sometime back I got in a fite wid dat negur, Frank Henderson, and he dun bit off dis heah ear yuh see in dis heah gode of salt. Now, suh, Marse Jeems, if yuh is de longest liber, and I jes' nose you gwine to be, I jes' want you, please, to promise' me dat yo' will see dis heah year put in de coffin 'long wid me when I am dead. 'Kase, suh, 'fore Gawd, I do'sn't want to be walkin' de golden streets ob Heaven wid one of my ears dun' bit off."

Here the old man broke down and could go no further, terribly distressed at the idea of being disfigured with one ear gone (or the better part of it) forever in Heaven. As I withdrew I promised him I would do as he requested. Alas, alas, the golden ties which bound us together so closely and so tenderly were rudely broken by the stern arbitrament of war. I greatly fear the dear old man was put away in his coffin without the comfort of carrying with him both of his ears to the general resurrection. Thus you see how carefully educated the old man had been by his old mistress in the doctrine of a bodily resurrection.

CHAPTER XII.

Forms of Entertainment.

SOME years had elapsed since the incidents of the last chapter. Over and often had the present writer enjoyed the companionship of Uncle Jim and Uncle Amos in their forays after fish and squirrels, taking his lessons in the various forms of woodcraft from these faithful ones, so willing, so capable of imparting them. He had also been carefully taught by Cicero, the coachman, how to hold the reins in driving, in such manner as, by the simple turn of the wrist of the left hand, the spirited team of ponies could be safely and (as the writer began to natter himself) gracefully driven, while the right hand was free to hold the whip, with its bow of pink ribbon tied about half way on the staff. To the two sons of the planter the faithful teacher and companion, the cultured, scholarly young Scotchman, the A.M. of the University of Edinburgh, Scotland, whose acquaintance we have already made, had given such faithful instruction at home as, with their rapid growth, made it necessary that they should be sent away to school. Pending the years of faithful scholastic guardianship we had come to love our master of the schoolroom, who devoted himself to us in many ways. In many respects he was among the most winsome, lovable persons whom the writer has ever met. With a face of fine intelligence, a voice naturally sweet, his vowel sounds in conversation or reading were singularly effective, and at times surcharged with such telling pathos as, for example, in reading aloud the "Heart of Midlothian," or some other of the blessed products of Sir Walter Scott, during a winter's evening around the blazing hearthstone of our happy home, would wet our young eyes with tears in loving sympathy with the annals of dear old Scotia. The name of this intellectual, pure minded, warm hearted young Scotchman was the same as that by him borne in the after years of his high distinction and marked pre-eminence among the divines of the South—Rev. James Melsey Sprunt, D.D. He has been gathered unto his fathers, but before he went away from among us, by the purity of his life, his ripe and full scholarship—but above all and in all, by his loyalty to God—he had so fully impressed his personality upon his pupils, such as the present Clerk of the North Carolina Supreme Court, Col. Thomas S. Kenan, and the Rev. J. D. Hufham, D.D., pastor, pastorum,[12] in the Baptist church, and many others, as has enabled them to honor God in serving their fellow men right royally. We shall never hear his rich, rolling Scotch voice again, in this life, as with rhythmic melody he read to the congregation "Guide Me, Oh, Thou Great Jehovah," but we hope to hear it again, with all his old pupils gathered around, in that blessed "house not made with hands, eternal in the Heavens." This tribute to the memory of one so worthy has been paid, not only because it is eminently due him, but to show also how careful the old planters of the South were in the selection of the teachers of their children. The elder brother of the writer went from his home to Princeton College in company with quite a number of young men from the neighboring town of New Berne. This town was so named in the latter part of the seventeenth century by its founder, Christopher Baron de Graffenreid,[13] in memory of his former home, Berne, in Switzerland. The writer went to the famous preparatory school in

[12] genitive plural of pastor

[13] Christoph von Graffenried (1661 – 1743) was the leader of an assemblage of Swiss and Palatine Germans to North Carolina in British North America in 1705. He later authored Relation of My American Project, a story of the founding of New Bern.

Orange County, North Carolina, kept by Mr. William I. Bingham, and since kept up by his descendants, on a high plane of great usefulness in developing the scholarship of the South.

We were both at home now, accompanied by several of our classmates, who were spending the vacation with us. The old home was full of young company, as our sisters had brought home with them some of their fair young schoolmates from St. Mary's School for Young Ladies, Raleigh, North Carolina. This remarkable institution was then, as now, perhaps the most popular school in the South. As well to welcome as to gladden our guests from a distance some of our special friends, boys and girls, had come out from Wilmington and New Berne, as they often did when the country was particularly inviting in its leafy and flowery pride; or in winter time, when the wild turkeys were ripe and the oysters were fat. One can quite understand to what height of real pleasure and loving forms of genuine enjoyment this carnival of old-fashioned fun and frolic should have risen in the old home in those blessed old days, before the flood of 1861 and 1865, under those conditions. It is true we had no bicycling parties then. What need, pray, had we for them, when the young people of that day had still their ancestral fondness for horseback riding—when the young ladies had not broken down and destroyed their gracefulness of carriage, but walked along corridor and through broad hall in all the mazes of the quadrille, Lancers and Scotch and Virginia reel with their peculiar grace of body, constituting them indeed the embodied poetry of motion? It would be very hard to say what sort of parties were not enjoyed by this half score and more of young people then gathered at the old home. Look out from the front piazza to the left at the horse block. What young couple is that about to mount those two beautiful horses for the ride out to the Sulphur springs three miles away? Wait until the family carriage and the lighter ones have been packed full of young people for the same delightful destination.

"Come, Buck, hurry up and get off as soon as you can, with your big hamper basket of lunch; and fill your wagon full of those largest watermelons and cantaloupes down there in the spring house."

"Yas, suh, Marse John; dat I will."

Well, all things are ready and off we go, as merry a party as ever kept time to music or read their destinies in each other's soft eyes; making the air vocal with the strains of fine melody, as the words of "Annie Laurie" went forth from the young people all along the line of mounted couples and from those in the carriages, which had joined the party at the main entrance—all en route to the Sulphur springs. These six or eight carriages full of bright, sunny faces untouched by cares or tears, as yet, with that peculiar, chaste toilet of the Southern girl, with their broad sunbonnets shading a type of beauty (in many cases) so marked as to have touched the heart of sternest recluse. Six or eight couples on horseback were keeping the regulation distance from each other, so that no one should suffer from dust or shadow of molestation in any form; while in the rear came the two or more wagons laden with dinner enough for a company of infantry, as well as melons, peaches, pears and baskets of Scuppernong grapes. Even now at the close of the nineteenth century, with all its multiplied cares and vexations of electric life, what an inspiration there is in youth. But to have been young in the dear old Southland in the fifties—no one but he who can speak of such joys as a blessed participant ought to be allowed to speak of them except in the reverent language of "Our fathers have declared it unto us what noble works thou didst in their days and in the old time before them." A quick drive of three miles brings us to the spring, though we stop a few minutes to see if Eli and Sam with their fiddles, Virgil with his flute, Frank with his banjo, Caswell with his triangle and Peter with his castanets had gone on. We were not detained long at the lake, for we found "dat Marse John and G'o'ge (George) had rid' on ahed." (rode on ahead.) Reaching the rendezvous, at the foot of quite a declivity for this flat

120

country, we find in this spring one of the very strongest fountains of medicinal water in this state. It breaks out from the side of a hill, in a volume of crystal water, about ten feet deep and as many in width, forming a deep basin, in which might float with perfect ease two or three pilot boats such as they employ in going to sea across the bar at Beaufort Harbor. Ah, dear old spring, what blessed memory, what Heaven recorded association, what fine forms of sweet hospitality cling to thy name! On the east bank of the purling little stream, which flows away from this bay of water, is a space cleared of all undergrowth, around the semi-circular rim of which are lined the fifteen or twenty carriages and a number of Concord wagons. In the center of this space there has been erected a platform about twenty-five feet square, while at one end is a stand with seats for the "musicianers," as Buck insists on calling them. Here and there, scattered about on the ground, with a thin layer of pine straw underneath, are buffalo robes, skins of wild animals, rugs and afghans, with such an array of cushions taken from the carriages as to suggest an Oriental siesta. The maid servants, who have come out in the lunch wagons, are very busy, rolling lemons on the hard seats of the wagons stripped of their cushions. Out on the edge of the woods where the horses have been hitched to young trees, but at a safe distance, have been kindled two or three fires, on which are placed the boilers brought in thoughtful reference to that delightful beverage, coffee, which the Southern cook brews in its highest perfection. Up the ravine some quarter of a mile away, the large party of young people have gone on one of those suggestive, rambling, philandering expeditions, to look for the old empty basin, from which one night, this fine spring near is said to have disappeared and broken out where in all of its limpid purity it is still flowing on. There is a legend about this old spring—that it belonged to a close fisted old man, who allowed himself to be annoyed by the many visitors who came for miles around to enjoy the water. The old curmudgeon boarded it up tight and fast with a close fence ten feet in height. One night the old man went to sleep the possessor of this spring, thus secured to him without annoyance. Next morning he awoke, but his spring had gone from him and his meanness forever. While the young people were gone on their ramble various dispositions for the pleasure of the party had been made by "Marse John" and the carriage drivers. Grapevines, as long as necessary and larger than your thumb, had been cut away from the large trees and with them were constructed primitive swings; cushions had been arranged with packs of playing cards on the central one, suggestive of whist, old maid, seven up, cribbage and the like; while backgammon boards were brought out from the wagon. Here they come—here they come.

"Eli, let us have a little music right away!"

"Yas, suh, dat we will, wid all pleasure', suh."

Soon the air was vocal with the suggestive notes of the old-fashioned dance music of:

"Hush, Miss Betsey, doan' you cry,

Your sweetheart will come by and by;

When he comes he'll come in blue,

To let you know his lub am true."

And then the chorus, in which the fine voices of the Negro musicians would ring out in perfect time with the instruments:

"Sheep shell corn by the rattle of his horn,

Send to the mill by the whip-poor-will."

As the inspiring notes of the sable orchestra reached the ears of the party, now returning from their ramble (in such suggestive subdivisions of two and two) they certainly did quicken their pace, for this band of happy youths knew what it all meant. They knew all the signs of the dance and all about it, in those days, when it was not unusual to see three generations of the same family in the same set; when the healthful mind and conscience recognized the fact that the majority of people commit forty times more sin with their tongues than they do with their toes; when the blessed differentiation was made between "piosity" (as Bishop Williams of Connecticut happily expresses it) and piety—

122

between goodishness and godliness. Can you think of a young partridge learning to run in the grass wet with the morning dew? Can you think of a young duck being taught to swim? Then you are in the frame of mind to be taught how and where the young people of the South learned to dance, and ride on horseback. Under the laws of heredity, these accomplishments came to them in the nursery. The present writer remembers learning to read and to write, but he does not remember learning to ride his pony or to dance. But what are we doing? This is not the time to indulge in an essay. Listen to old Eli's voice, as he sways his body in unison with his deep interest in what now engages him, calling out in a strong voice:

"Pardners for de fus' cotillion."

How rapidly the set fills up! How strange it is that the same couples that came down the ravine together just now appear together on the platform! Ah, as Eli draws the long notes on his instrument and calls out, "honors to yo' pardners," what graceful curtsies, what stately (but not stiff) bows are those, flinging contempt on the cold, icy, mechanical forms of the modern German, as "Forward fours" starts the couple on the round of the old-fashioned cotillion of the better days of the republic. Watch the features of that sweet-hearted young Carolinian, who is not in this set, but is biding his time and waiting his turn, as by the glow in his eyes he is calling out in his poetic soul:

"On with the dance, let joy be unconfined,
No sleep till morn, when youth and beauty meet
To chase the glowing hours with flying feet."

Set after set is danced and no indication of fatigue. You might just as well endeavor to fatigue an Arabian courser as one of these young gentlemen in the dance. You might as well try to break down with fatigue a fair antelope of the plains as one of these beautiful girls. Ah, children of a happy day, with whom no coming events casts its dark shadow before, go on, go on with your blessed round of innocent joy—the cloud no bigger than a man's hand, and yet flecked with blood, has not yet cast its

123

shadow across your bright pathway! And as they dance on, with couples resting, not because they are fatigued but to give others their places, what are Buck and his Marse John doing, pray? They are beginning to take the melons out of the cool pool of the spring water, in which, in large sacks, they have been held down by long poles fastening them to the bottom. This seems to be the signal for dinner. Yes, but what rumbling of wheels is that we hear?

"B'ess my life an' soul an' body, honey," one of the servants calls out, "if it ain't old Marster and ole Mistiss dun drive out to spend' de day in honor ob Marse John's burfda'." (birthday)

That was the state of the case. Presently the maids sweep off the platform, which is soon covered by snow white table linen, and then how rapidly all the appointments for an excellent dinner are made—with knives and forks and snowy napkins and, in fact, everything necessary—none will doubt, save those ignorant of the fine service and good taste of the old plantation dining room servants, who were out to-day in numbers to have the pleasure of making "Marse John berry happy on his burfda'." (birthday) No attempt to describe that dinner will be made. Suffice it to say that cold meats—ham, lamb, beef, chicken and venison, with tomatoes and such vegetables as could be served cold, and all that anyone could desire—were there in such abundance as left no one present, servant and all, even to dear old faithful Buck, with any suggestion of an aching void, but in such plenty as to suggest, yes, exemplify:

"One continued feast of nectared sweets,
  Where no crude surfeit reigns."

After the melons had been cut, true Southern fashion, lengthwise into halves, with a spoon, they were greatly enjoyed, as each person industriously betook himself to this delicious Southern fruit. After the decks were cleared dancing was resumed. Nothing would do with the young people on such a red letter day as that of the birthday of their eldest son but that father and mother should join in the first set after dinner. One

124

could readily see how these two dear old people had not been neglected in the matter of polite education in the early part of their lives. Eight merrily did these two dear old folks enter into the pleasures of the young people, "in their hands all around," "swing corners," "forward four," and "promenade all," in such a manner as to reflect credit on their old French dancing master in the first decade of the century. Besides this they have been in the habit of brightening the home life by joining with their children in all the innocent pastimes of the nursery. At the South dancing was among them. Martin Luther, in the sixteenth century, taught the people of Germany to elevate the morals of their children by making their homes happy. The short criminal dockets of that favored land clearly indicate how singularly successful that remarkable man was. So says Marlitt, in his novel of "Gold Elsie," and others. As to everything on this earth there must be an end, so after an hour or more of delightful enjoyment everything was packed up, horses were hitched and saddled, and this party of light-hearted folk made their way homeward singing out in loud, clear and sweet voices the Canadian boat song "Row, brothers, row." Just as the hunter's full moon, coming up through the tall trunks of the fine old pines east of the old home, was beginning to flood the whole landscape with that touch of unearthly beauty peculiar to our Southern latitude, on our left, as we were driving up the front entrance, from the arbor of a Scuppernong grapevine were heard the sweet notes of the mocking-bird pouring out his roundelay of love to his mate, rejoicing over their young brood. Very soon we heard the deep voice of old "Don," the faithful Newfoundland. Just then a young gentleman from Wilmington, in full sympathy with this charming scene, evidenced his appreciation in clear, rich musical voice:

"'Tis sweet to hear the honest watchdog's bark,
    Bay deep-mouthed welcome, as we draw nigh home;
    'Tis sweet to know there is an eye that marks our coming,
    And grows brighter when we come.

125

But sweeter than this, than these, than all,
  Is first and passionate love;
  It stands alone, like Adam's recollection of his fall."

Just then the young couple we saw riding away on Horseback this morning came up. They were singularly silent, notably so the young gentleman, who, after assisting the young lady to dismount, made his way in silence to my brother John's room. Left alone, he caught up a pen and in the intensity of his deep feeling showed clearly how busy the blind little god, Cupid, had been that day, as he wrote:

"Who breathes must suffer; who thinks must mourn;
  He alone is blessed who ne'er was born."

He went out for some purpose, and soon thereafter our brilliant young neighbor, Tom Wilson, entered the room. He saw the paper with the above lines lying on the writing table, the ink still wet, left there in the writer's unconscious abstraction, and wrote currente calamo.

"Not so; all good men rugged paths have trod,
  And stiffening renders man more worthy of God."

Thus ended an old-fashioned field day with its band of most interesting Southern youth. The question will come up, "Where are they all now?" and echo, for answer, gives back in sepulchral tones, "Where! Oh, where?"

CHAPTER XIII.

An Excursion to the sea.

WITH his house full of young company, the old planter and his wife the next day planned an excursion to the seaside, commonly known, in the parlance of the coastal South, as a "pony-penning;" in full preparation for which he dispatched a trusted servant with a letter to Mr. Robert McClane, the old Scotch host at Swansboro, the little seaport in the south-east corner of the good old county of Onslow, some thirty miles away, asking him to have sail boats in readiness to take the party through Rogue Sound to Beaufort, suggesting that it would add to the pleasure of his guests if he himself would go along, and would he be pleased to see that every detail was in perfect order? The day intervening was spent by the young people in the manner customary on the large estates—in fishing, hunting, riding and driving, while some time was expended by the young ladies in helping the mistress, their hostess, with work on a silk quilt already in the frame. In the evening the young people of both sexes who had been invited to join the excursion dropped into tea without ceremony, and the time passed away most delightfully until the hour for retiring came, with games of whist, dancing and music, and by some in those suspicious rambles about the flower garden that suggest the lines of the English poet, when he said in a note to his lovely sweetheart:

"Too late I stayed, forgive the crime,
  Unheeded passed the hours,
For noiseless falls the foot of time
  When it only treads on flowers."

Next morning, after a good old-fashioned breakfast, amply supplied with transportation for themselves, servants and luggage, through the unvarying kindness of the neighboring planters, the large party were off to the seaside, the accomplished wife of a young planter gladly going along as chaperone. The road led over a very level country, with little or no sand in the roadbed. Thus in six hours from the time of leaving, that is about the middle of the afternoon, the party were kindly received by old Bobby McClane at his sweet hostelry, where dinner was soon served, and long before sunset we were embarked for the run by moonlight down the Sound to the seaside. The wind was fair and strong enough to carry us rapidly, with the tide all right, over this beautiful sheet of water, flowing in ample breadth for fine sailing, like a land locked lake, with the narrow Rogue banks between us and the ocean. What mirth provoking anecdotes, what rich voices in fine old song, of the "Irish Emigrant's Lament," "Make Me No Gaudy Chaplet," "Way Down on the Suwanee River," and others, with guitar, violin and flute. What mirth provoking and at the same time engaging badinage, as our fine boats were cleaving their way through the phosphorescent, moonlit waters, the present writer will not attempt to tell, but they are all deeply engraved on memory's tablets, there to endure as long as she is faithful to her sweet trust.

ANNOTATION: Here are the lyrics to "The Irish Emigrant's Lament," which are in the public domain.

THE IRISH EMIGRANT'S LAMENT

Och! while I live I'll never forget
The troubles of that day,
When bound into a foreign land
Our ship got under way.
My friends I left at Belfast town,
My love at Carrick shore,

And I gave to poor old Ireland
My blessing o'er and o'er.
Och! well I knew as off we sailed,
What my hard fate would be;
For, gazing on my country's hills
They seemed to fly from me.
I watched them as we sailed away
Until my eyes grew sore,
And I felt that I was doomed to walk
The Shamrock sod no more.
They say I'm now in freedom's land,
Where all men masters be;
But were I in my winding-sheet
There's none to care for me.
I must, to eat the strangers bread,
Abide the stranger's scorn,
Who taunts me with thy dear loved name
Sweet isle, where I was born.
Och! Where — Och! Where's the careless heart
I once could call my own?
It bade a long farewell to me
The day I left Tyrone.
Not all the wealth by hardship won
Beyond the Western main,
Thy pleasures, my own absent home,
Can bring to me again.

From John Ord, *Ord's Bothy Songs and Ballads*, pp. 352-353.

http://mudcat.org/@displaysong.cfm?SongID=9772

One, however, may be quite sure, that one has reached that
sweet era in life, when silence is golden. It is long after midnight,
after a glorious run, without an accident of any kind, that the
gruff voice of old Caesar Manson, captain of one of the fine boats,

the Etta Duncan, rang out, as we stood away from where Morehead City now stands, across the lovely Beaufort harbor.

"When young eyes look love to eyes that speak again,
And all goes merry as a marriage bell,"
"Haul aft the mainsheet and let her come about."
"What light is that on our right bow?"
"That is the light of the Fort Macon lighthouse and the one here away on the weather bow is at the Atlantic Hotel."
"Let her come around."

And in a short time the voice of our kindly host, Mr. Pender, was heard at his wharf, welcoming old Bobby McClane who had come along with the party. In a few minutes we were all stowed away in comfortable quarters, all ready for us, for had not the old Scotchman sent ahead and given mine host of the Atlantic ample notice of our coming? I wish, reader, you could have seen that supper, which the Edgecombe hospitality had so abundantly provided or, better still, if only we could partake of it now. Fish, oysters, clams, scallops and crabs, all of the rich products of salt water, with that remarkable and best sauce of all, salt water appetite, which "waits upon good digestion." Will you believe it, at eight o'clock the next morning breakfast was not only ready but we were ready for breakfast, young ladies and all? By ten o'clock all the dispositions for the trip to the Banks had been made, but the weather showing up rather rough, it was deemed most prudent that the ladies should remain at the hotel. Off we went in quite a large centerboard craft, in nautical classification known as a "lighter," the significance of which term this deponent sayeth not for to some of the Piedmontese and mountaineers on board (we had not gone far when it became exceedingly rough) in fact to many of our largely increased party, the depression of spirits attendant on sea-sickness was anything else than a lighting up of joy. The writer remembers well that on this "pony penning" expedition were two persons who later in life became distinguished—Honorable Thomas L. Clingman,[14]

130

afterwards United States Senator of North Carolina, and Mr. Edmond Ruffin of Virginia, the latter of whom it is said fired the first gun at Fort Sumter.

It is generally doubted whether either of these gentlemen ever became quite as sick of secession and its sequela as they became that day, in a roost moving way, of the loblolly motion of boat and sea and air—of earth and heaven. What a fiend is this seasickness! Well, here we are in just the position to get a good view of the large crowds assembled to witness the penning of these ponies. The island is a long, narrow one, of the many that flank the coast here, and which from Hatteras, north and south, render navigation so dangerous. Many think these ponies are the increase of horses, which escaped from settlers in colonial days. The diminished size, constituting them ponies, is the outcome of interbreeding and the short rations of coarse marsh grass without grain. The fisherman and others who own these islands pen the ponies twice each year, at which time the colts are branded and a sale takes place. Among the many driven into these pens (led along through the gap of a decoy, in the shape of an animal already domesticated) one can find almost any color desired. Some of them are well shaped, requiring only the good feed and careful grooming they will get as companions of the young people on estates inland, and, in some cases, in the Piedmont and mountain counties. The average price is forty

[14] Thomas Lanier Clingman (1812 –1897), known as the "Prince of Politicians," was a (Democratic) Congressman (HR) from 1843 to 1845 and from 1847 to 1858, and U.S. senator from the state of North Carolina from 1858 until 1861. At the onset of the Civil War he obstinately refused to resign his Senate seat and was one of the ten senators who were ejected from the Senate in "absentia." He went on to become a general in the Confederate States Army. This work is in the public domain in the United States because it is a work prepared by an officer or employee of the United States Government as part of that person's official duties under the terms of Title 17, Chapter 1, Section 105 of the US Code.

dollars; indeed it is said that this is the fixed price, as corn and fodder cost nothing here and the owners refuse to accept a smaller amount. The penning is over with all of its chaffering and bargaining, with all the kicking and biting and vicious squealing of these unbridled animals; the purchasers have supplied themselves and we are quite ready to go. Although the weather was rough, very rough, nothing of special note occurred on the homeward voyage. Our friends at the hotel in Beaufort had quite enjoyed the day with its trip to old Fort Macon, and the fine fishing on the wharf, while some of the party had enjoyed that luxury even greater than the far famed Turkish bath—a splash in the wild, wild waves of old ocean as they come tumbling in on the fine beach of this charming seaside resort. Next morning, bright and early, our boats were brought into requisition and we made fine progress on our homeward trip. Reaching Swansboro after a delightful run, the carriages were soon made ready and we were ere route for the old plantation, which we reached in good time, after a delightful jaunt, which lived in the memory of all who made up this party of joyous, sunny-hearted youths of a generation passed away. We knew we violated no law of hospitality as we drove up the broad avenue of the old homestead singing, at the top of our voices, "Home Again From a Foreign Shore," for were not the lights still burning in the old home and in the dear hearts of the old father and mother? Alas, alas, these blessed lights have gone out forever, and the darkness following is so great as to blind with tears the eyes, rapidly misting over, of the author as he pens these lines. Hail and farewell, blessed ones of the past! Hail and farewell!

CHAPTER XIV.

Excitement of the arrival of a circus in the area.

WE ALL regard it as part of the good fortune, which in those days seemed to wait upon youth that flaming hand bills and immense posters of a circus and menagerie were abroad in the land at that time, and that the old Robinson and Eldred people of the sawdust and trapeze would soon delight our community. Everybody far and near was discussing the oncoming circus, with its telling opiate to conscience, that fine study of natural history commonly known in church circles as a menagerie, with no suggestion of enjoyment in the circus (?). Through Uncle Philip and the foremen on the plantation, orders had been given for a full holiday in every department of the industries of the estate. Even Uncle Amos, the plantation Nimrod, had been told that ole Marster had bought a ticket for his whole family, black and white, and that the roll would be called by Marse John in front of Ben's house at ten o'clock, on the ringing of the assembly bell. Ben had been ordered to have transportation in readiness, consisting of all the wagons and carts from the lake, together with everything of like order on the plantation. It was scarcely necessary to give an order that everybody should appear in their best clothes, for the racial pride of our servants, not to say anything of their family or plantation pride, would be very sure to suggest this. At this late day one can scarcely appreciate the strength of family pride among the servants on one of the best-managed plantations of that day. So strong was it that, in case of a marriage of one of their number to a servant belonging to a family not the social equal of their master, you would be sure to hear some harsh criticisms from the blue-black aristocrats, reprobating such conduct in terms so strong as to make its occurrence infrequent. Aunt Dinah with an emphatic toss of her turbaned head, and a tinge of bitter scorn in her voice would say:

"Dat negur, Sam, gwine to fling hisself 'way anyhow; marrying' dat common negur gal, Mary Jane. Her white folkses ain't no quality nohow fur nothin'.'"

In political campaigns, especially for the local or county officers, where these people, as elsewhere, had neither voice nor vote—when party strife ran high, and high it did run, in those days of joint discussion—one would have been amusingly surprised to have witnessed their deep interest in politics, often wagering as high as a half dozen coon skins on the result of the election. No one ought to be surprised when told that most of these servants on those manorial estates were old-fashioned Whigs; for was not the institution of slavery a strong breakwater, protecting in its conservatism the South and the country against any forms of anarchical radicalism?

Be this as it may, circus day came around and everybody was ready for this high carnival of fun and frolic. The writer heartily wishes that you and he, kind reader, could go back and witness the gathering of the "family," at the time appointed, when the loud notes of the assembly bell rang out all along Broadway and Chestnut streets, while the servants began to gather in the large area just to the right of Ben's house. The writer witnessed it but cannot describe it. And yet (as the wagons, ox carts and horse carts are falling into line and Uncle Philip, mounted on Selim, is discharging the important duties of marshal, in ordering the women and children to mount the vehicles, whose bottoms have been heavily covered with soft wheat straw) you must take time to look at Ben a few minutes. Did you ever see anyone quite so happy as he is to-day with his best clothes on? Look at that tall fur hat (it was before the common use of the silk hat), and notice his proud movements, as with pride in his mien and step, he takes a big bandanna handkerchief out of the depths of his long-skirted, claw-hammer coat pocket. His coat is of blue broadcloth, with metal buttons almost as large as a half dollar, and just as bright as chalk and friction can make them, while his black pants and canary-colored waistcoat, with bright colored stockings encased in patent leather shoes, make up his outfit entire, except that flaming red cravat. Ah, never was there a happier "Negro" on earth than faithful Ben, whom his Marse John had just dressed up in a suit of his own clothes; nor will his joy and gladness be surpassed when the millennium comes. Here come the carriages full of fresh-hearted young people from the great house, with ole Marster and ole Missus, and the young people on horseback, with Handy driving the baggage wagon full of maid servants, and the old gardener. Marse John, riding on that beautiful sorrel, with that fair and graceful young lady, superbly mounted, led the way, followed by as happy a set of devoted servants as ever gladdened the hearts or enriched the purse of a typical young planter. On they go, some four or five miles away, to the little hamlet of Upper Rich Lands, across the river on the road towards the old town of New Berne.

Without accident to anyone of the large party, safe arrival is made on the circus ground. My sakes! What a crowd. It would appear as though the whole of the upper part of Onslow and the lower part of Jones counties were here to-day. Such crowds of people, white and black, the air ringing out with the loud guffaws of laughter, rich and deep; such instances of marked attention from the ebon beaux to the dusky belles; such a flow of big "bookionary" words as were then and there employed, with certain other forms of speech, not so loud nor so articulate, yet fully understood; for who has ever yet mistaken Cupid's dialect? Ah, Ben was in his glory that day, and so was Uncle Philip; while if you could have seen my man Cain, "gallivanting" with Julia and Edith, the house maids, you would have regarded him as in a frame of mind truly enviable; for there are certain forms of earthly happiness just as contagious as whooping cough or measles. Well, the doors are open and the plantation people are filing past Marse John, who is standing by the door-keeper, keeping his tally to see that all entitled (and no more) under the

135

family ticket are allowed to go in. My sakes! what a revelation to these hundreds of dusky toilers did this entrance make. Talk no more to me of Aladdin's lamp! These children of Africa had entered another world. Happy! That is not the word. Simply enchanted. If you could have seen Buck's eyes when the band of music (trombone and all) broke forth you would have said, as their white eyes rolled around in ecstasy, "Happier is he by far to-day than if he were eating 'possum' and 'taters.'" They roamed around the large pavilion, looking at the various animals—elephants, camels, bears, hyenas, tigers, leopards, rhinoceros and others, and you would have observed that all the ox cart drivers were together. There they were —Harry, Isaac, Handy, Tom and Sam—obeying the unwritten guild-law of human life. On they went leisurely until they reached the place where stood the giraffe. There they stood as if chained to the spot by the paralyzing power of dumb admiration. There they stood and looked and looked, until at last old Handy, rolling his big "chaw" of tobacco in his cavernous mouth and shooting a sharp elbow in among Harry's short ribs, called out, with a loud laugh:

"Look heah, negur, how do yuh think dat ting (pointing to the giraffe) ebber (ever) git up when he dun git down. His hind legs am so much shorter dan his fore legs?"

This was a poser. They could not compass the answer. At which they laughed and laughed, moving on at the same time with the crowd until they came to the corner where the monkeys were chained on the top of the cages of the larger animals. Here again they stopped. They gazed in silence at these connecting links (as some affirm) between the two orders of animal life. At last, when the laughable grimaces of one of the monkeys broke the spell of their dumb amazement, old Handy the wit of the party, spoke up:

"Yuh see dem monkeys up dere? Dey is mi'ty cuirisum (curious) critters ennyhow; dat big monkey up dere, way back in yonder? He's got lots of sense,—an'—an'—he kin talk, too. Duz yo' know why he don't talk? 'Case he jes' fairly 'nos' ef he talks de white fokeses set him to work rite away—dat's why he doan' talk."

Well, after this colloquy between these two old darkies, and half an hour or so had been allowed for the inspection of all the animals, the time came for the ring master and the clown to perform their part—the trained dogs and the acting elephant, the bareback riders, the various astounding feats of acrobats, with the man who wound himself up in his somersaults, and all that is so familiar to those who remember with pleasure this hour and more of abandon to the enjoyment of the circus, it was announced by the ring master that the celebrated lion tamer would now appear in his world-renowned act of driving the magnificent Libyan lion, Nero, in his chariot. There immediately followed a breathless silence, and none were more attentive or silent than the hundreds of servants, who were drinking in everything with eyes, ears and open mouths. Presently the lion tamer entered Nero's cage with his whip in his hand, ready to harness up this monarch of the forest, when, to the dismay of all who heard it, there was a suppressed angry growl from the lion. The keeper, nothing daunted, advanced toward the animal, careful to keep his back to the door by which he had entered the cage, with his keen, magnetic eye fastened upon the sullen king of the jungle. No one knows what caused it, whether it was the presence of so many servants, suggestive to the lion of his home and freedom in Africa or not, but in a moment there was a deep roar from Nero and a half spring toward the keeper, and the rattling as of a link or two of an iron chain fastened to the end of a club, with which the keeper struck the lion with great force between the eyes, followed by a fearful growl from the infuriated animal. Just then someone called out:

"He is killing his keeper, he is breaking out; he is breaking out!"

In all your life you never saw such a scene. In less time than is required to tell of it there was the most fearful confusion confounded. Crash, crash, crash went the seats; rip, rip went the

137

canvas; as the panic-stricken crowd, not standing on the order of their going, tore their way through the large tent out into the open air. Anywhere, any way to escape; as someone crazed with fear called out in tones unmistakable:

"De lion is loose! De lion is loose! Lord hab mercy! Lord hab mercy!"

My sakes, what a scene. Fortunately the white people were not so much crazed by fear. The Negroes were wild, and it is said that in their rapid, crazy flight some never called a halt until they had crossed the river, in their fearful, crazy hurry to get home. Among those who led this wild flight was poor Buck, who never afterwards could bear to talk of the circus. He had enough, and much preferred the coon hunt as his mode of enjoyment. It turned out that while this incident broke up the performance, the lion had been so stunned by the blow as to enable the keeper to escape. Not many months, however, after this noted event in the simple annals of the plantation the newspapers announced that Nero had killed his foolhardy keeper out in Indiana. We all reached home in safety, and as we sat down to dinner many were the jokes told and incidents related. The truth demands that, all-in-all, the second edition of the circus, while discussing a good dinner, was far more enjoyable than the one in the morning, with its dangerous fiasco and ludicrous stampede of the African race from the circus for home and safety. The old planter gave his servants, however, a delightful day, notwithstanding this amusing episode.

CHAPTER XV.

Rapid increase of the African race in the South prior to 1865 — Majority of the Southern planters took good care of their servants — because it paid off to do so. Plantation amusements for Negroes.

WE HAVE seen that the proprietor of this estate sought successfully, to secure rather a willing than enforced obedience to the rules and regulations of the plantation. This he did by a wise system of rewards for high usefulness in special cases, and by a kind and well-nigh paternal oversight over all his servants. Recognizing the fact that these people were his property, the regime was one of unbroken kindness, with the fact clearly certified that disobedience invariably brought its own penalty. Kind, yet firm, his servants were fully conscious of the fact that certainty rather than severity of penalty was the active deterrent to disobedience. On a large plantation like this the system or order was the outcome of established laws, which were well known to his people from cradledom in the great majority of cases. In the earlier part of his life, following the example of many planters around him, he had employed white overseers; but as he went on in life's lessons of experience and wisdom he found that with this white element around him there devolved upon him the double labor of managing the overseers as well as the servants. From the lower class of whites, not the lowest, the overseers of the South were recruited. Out of sympathy with the Negroes, they were simply and solely white drivers, in contract with the planter, the practical working of which relation was, that for the first year it was the planter's estate, the second year it was a joint stock establishment—in the estimation of the overseer—who acted the third year as though the planter, plantation and all belonged to him. Coming from that element in which morale was largely lacking, it was ascertained that they could not be relied upon for the most healthful forms of discipline and good, wholesome government on the plantation. Therefore it was that for many years on this estate the system of colored managers or foremen had displaced the less reliable order of overseers. This was found in many respects to be far preferable, and notably so in that it maintained the closest private relations between the planter and his servants. In one sense they were *all servants together*; and to the most sensible of the servants it soon became apparent that, in those close bonds of confidence and interest, the old master and the old mistress were indeed the veriest slaves on the estate, in those severe exactions of time, patience and watchful energy, with affection supplied by them to those whom they could not but recognize as so many overgrown children. Hence it was that Uncle Philip was commissioned as next in authority to the planter, while Uncle Jim, Uncle Suwarro, Ben and Cicero, each had their department, with their full share of discipline and responsibility, all centering in the owner of the estate. In all the relations of life no system to which man puts his pitchy fingers has been found perfect, while experience has taught that the management of the plantation, with its better crops, fewer instances of punishment and more harmonious working of the Negro, the foreman regime was a marked improvement over the white overseer. In those days the curse of the plantation life was in the constant temptation of the servants, coming from the hurtful influence of small stores, kept by the lower class of whites. These people were ready, by night, to carry on a system of demoralizing barter, taking at their own price articles stolen by the servants, to wit, corn, poultry, pigs; in short, anything the Negro might carry in his bag, in any sense marketable; in exchange for which mean whiskey or other articles at high prices to compensate for the great risk they took, were sold to the servants. Those dens, while exceedingly harmful, were ordinarily short lived in the hands of any one of these midnight enemies to the planter, who kept in his pay a spy on the movements of the lawless Negro traders. Few such cases went to the courts.

For mutual protection all the planters were closely banded together. As soon as well-grounded suspicion fell upon one of these establishments the keeper was waited upon by several of the planters. A fair price was offered in cash for his few acres and storeroom, and such emphatic notice to get out was given as suggested a coat of tar with a full ruffling of feathers. Within the designated forty-eight hours the man had decamped, bag and baggage, for he had a very healthy regard for Judge Lynch and the consequences of a trial in that form. Sometimes a year or more would elapse before another one of these deadfalls with its harmful nuisances sprang up, only to be abated in the same manner above indicated. Short lived as any one of them was, yet they were very annoying to the planter, while they were a prolific source of trouble to the servants. It may be well to say in this connection that while corporal punishment was resorted to in the maintenance of discipline, it was infrequent and never so severe as the same mode of punishment in the navy of the United States or any other well-ordered Government at that time. The more frequent mode of punishment was the curtailment of special privileges on Saturday afternoon and close, solitary confinement in the "lockup," as the servants called the small jail in the third story of the gin house. When any one of the servants insisted on incorrigible disobedience and none of the ordinary modes of punishment seemed to do any good, after every other expedient had been exhausted, he was sent away to that Botany Bay in the lower Mississippi valley, to work on the cotton plantations of that section of the South, where the commercial features of the earlier days of the institution had been in some sense revived, and where, in consequence, the patriarchal features, as seen in Virginia, Maryland and the Carolinas, had gone somewhat into abeyance.

So much for the discipline, penalties, punishment and restraints, which obtained on this estate. Something must be said

141

in regard to the care of the health of the servants. If one could have seen the large number of children under ten years of age on this estate, satisfactory answer would have been given to many questions which naturally enough arise in this connection. The almost daily visits paid by my mother to the bedside of the mothers of these children for a month (never less) after their birth; the facts of the food for them being carried from the planter's table thrice daily by Eliza, special maid to ole Mistiss; the regular visits of the plantation physician, a regular graduate in this case of either the University of Dublin, Ireland, in the person of the elder Dr. Duffy, or of the University of Pennsylvania, in the case of Dr. Christopher Whitehead, can account for the larger number of children coming on rapidly, to go to the plantation or turpentine industries when sufficiently old, than you would certainly find among any peasantry in the world.

These facts, which are carefully brought out, will explain the rapid increase of the African race in the South prior to 1865; while the absence of these conditions since then, together with the baneful effects on the Negroes of the South, coming from their close herding together in the towns and villages, have told on the comparative ratio of increase and healthfulness of the two periods. Leaving all questions of humanity and philanthropy out of view, the great majority of the Southern planters took good care of their servants, sick or well, precisely for the same reason that the farmers in the Genesee Valley in New York took special pains and went to adequate expense in the preparation of their fine wheat lands—because it paid to do so.

One may be interested to know something of the various amusements on the plantation. These sunny-hearted children of the equator, mercurial in their temperament, of ordinarily excellent health and, in their relation to the old planter, largely exempt from the "What shall I eat? What shall I wear?" carking cares of every-day life, were happy in their relations to the old master. To some, the problem of amusement or occupation out of labor hours may be thus stated: Eli given his fiddle, Sam with his banjo, and a room well sanded, twenty feet square, with Julia, Kate and fifteen or twenty others of the plantation girls, dressed up to kill—what time or cause had the beaux of the estate to inquire into the prices of anything to eat or to wear? Again, around at dear old Granddaddy Cain's house in the evening, with old Harper, the Baptist preacher, or Daniel, the Methodist exhorter, in fine voice or tune, with everything to urge them to the full enjoyment of a decided counterblast to the "double shuffle," "pigeon wing," or "reel," going on under the inspiration of Eli's fiddle, what, it may be asked, did they lack to their fullest enjoyment but the enlargement of all those spiritual privileges at the "sociashun" or the camp meeting, to which they were looking forward so joyously after harvest.

It was somewhat amusing to see in how many particulars the manners and customs of the planter's family were copied by their servants, so faithfully do we all show the power of environment. Did my mother have a silk quilt in the frame and invite some of her neighbors to assist her in finishing the same, in a short time a similar gathering at Aunt Daphne's or Aunt Peggy's might be seen during the long winter evenings, with the possum supper and a dance—with such peals of joyous laughter one might hear from this band of happy, well fed, well housed people. Then again, aside from the coon and possum hunts, there were many games, into the mysteries of which, down at the quarter, the plantation servants were inducted by the house servants of both sexes. They pitched quoits, ran foot races and played ball. With them a famous game was "bull pen," and still another was "roly-poly," in the playing of which many a young darky would receive a good rousing lick with the ball if he happened not to make good his distance from the set of holes in the ground. All were allowed to go fishing and some of the most careful, trusted ones went squirrel hunting while as a boy many and many a time did I take lessons from Caswell, as he taught me how to twist "bre'er rabbit" out of a hollow log or tree. One of their favorite

143

amusements was that of breaking a yoke of young steers or oxen. High fun it was when, with their tails tied together, these young bullocks would run away and clear themselves of the cart, young darkies and all, until at last, wearied out by a band of these young Africans, "Rock" and "Jake" would "jest 'habe demsel's (themselves) jes' lik' t'other oxens." My sakes, what fun they would have in breaking in a colt, be the same mule or horse! All these young Arabs would want was "Marster's 'mission," with a good stiff bit and plenty of plow line. Fall after fall might come, but they would persevere until they would break down the young animal's spirit, and then how happy they would be. Very frequently they would guard against the mules' racial disposition to buck by using a Bedouin bit and a wooden martingale. Thus outfitted they were not long "in brokin' dis heah mule." And yet with all these modes of spending their time, many of them would occupy themselves in the cultivation of their own crops and gardens; or else they might be seen with a large bundle of white oak splits or a basket of corn shucks making baskets, foot mats or horse collars.

My observation of the Negro leads me to think that he was, under the old regime, a far more industrious member of the family than he has been represented by many to have been. As we read in the Bible, "like priest like people," so an industrious planter was ordinarily blest with energetic and thrifty servants. It has been said so often that by many it is believed—if the average Negro on the plantation bore no malice, he was essentially lacking in gratitude. The writer is the product of the social forces of the old plantation days and can well claim an opinion on the subject in question. The Negroes that I knew and observed for over a quarter of a century, differed largely from that generation of their race that has come on since the war. The former, under the close association that was slowly yet surely elevating his race, was fully alive to the strong forces of gratitude, and showed too that he was wrought upon (and who is not, I would like to inquire?) by passion, by hate and by malice as well. The later products of the race, except in a few instances, have been steadily depreciating in all the finer elements of gratitude, truth, honesty, and industry. This is so necessarily. They have been from force of circumstances, chiefly political, directly antagonized to those from close association with whom there had been an imparting of much that was gradually lifting them up from paganism. Largely over a million of them had become members of the different Christian bodies in the South prior to 1861, and worshipped regularly with their owners around the same altars when God's holy day came around. On the estate here treated of they were mostly members of the Baptist and Methodist Churches. Nearly all of the older settled servants here belonged to one or the other of these two bodies while not a few of the younger ones were rejoicing in the comfort of that faith, touching the simplicity of which a wayfaring man, though a fool, need not err therein. The local colored preacher attended funerals on the plantation, burying their dead in the "God's Acre," set apart and religiously observed for that purpose. It was indeed a very rare occurrence for the name of one of the old plantation servants to appear on the criminal docket of our courts. Alas, alas, in these days it is the younger generation, the product of the enforced forms of liberty *before they were ready for it*, which claims the attention of the prosecuting officers and who swell the ranks of our overrun penitentiaries. The old-fashioned colored man to this day is not of the class whose lawless and brutish conduct brings on him the swift and unrelenting fate of fiends.

But this is the time for either argument. These have remorselessly passed. Yet upon many of the most thoughtful men of the country, it has already dawned as a frightful truth that if the sweeping manumission of the race was a mistake, their wholesale indiscriminate enfranchisement was a crime. So says the late United States Senator, Ingalls. We shall leave both crime and criminals of both sections of a common country to the avenging nemesis of history and hurry on with our recital of facts and incidents.

CHAPTER XVI.

A Negro wedding on the old plantation.

FOR SOME weeks prior to a plantation wedding there was always more or less of a buzz of comment, sometimes kind and just as often unkind. The turbaned African Mrs. Grundy would pass both the parties to the marriage in sharp review and settle whether Ben was "de negur for dat gal, Fanny, to marry." Even there, as in the far more conventional circles, there was a self-constituted high court of propriety, from whose opinion there was no appeal. Well, it is all fixed. Ben is to marry Fanny. "Ole Marster and ole Mistuss hab dun bin axed fur dere 'mission." Old Uncle Harper, the colored minister, has been notified. Supper (and such a supper) has all been arranged "in de white fokeses' kitchen." The groom, full of joy, has been in the hands of Marse John, and his wedding suit of clothes has been pronounced all right; while the young ladies of the family have given Fanny anything and everything necessary (from their full and well-appointed wardrobe) to make out a becoming outfit for this dusky bride. Have you never noticed how deep, how general, the interest is in all brides? Pitiable indeed is the nature that is not wrought upon by the sweetest sympathies and deepest interest in a woman, be she black or be she white, who has reached that pivotal point in her life, so full of mystery as to infuse an air of almost solemn reverence about all brides. The ceremony was performed in the large dining room of the family after the usual supper hour. There stood the old Negro preacher, dear old Uncle Harper, with his book in his hand, properly dressed up in a suit of black broadcloth, given him long years ago by old master, with his high white collar, strongly wrapped around by a broad white necktie, which was reaching for the base of his ears. Did you ever see such spectacles in your life, with such large glasses, broadly

rimmed around by an alloy of metals commonly known as brass
—very heavy and scoured very bright. All the white family were
there with packages in their hands, presents for the bride. The
broad veranda was full of servants, while some could not obtain
standing room there and were standing out in the yard. The
families of the bride and groom were invited into and ranged
around the dining room, leaving ample space for the bride and
groom. Presently from the keys of the piano sounded the joyous
notes of the wedding march, as the tapering fingers of Miss
Rebecca, fresh from St. Mary's School, gently yet artistically
touched the same. There was a deep hush of deeper expectancy,
when in walked Ben, with Fanny modestly leaning on his arm.
Not even Chauncey Depew, with his mirror-studied airs and
graces, could have been more imposing than his much beloved
brother Ben on this occasion; while the daughter of Jay Gould
could not have borne herself with more becoming grace or
modesty than did our African bride. Standing before Uncle
Harper in mute expectancy, the old man lifted up his rich,
mellow voice and asked:

"Who gibs (gives) dis 'oman to dis man?" when the bride's
father said:

"I doz."

Ben bowed very profoundly to him and said:

"I t'ank yuh, Uncle Peter, I curtenly doz."

Then the old preacher said:

"Ben, will yuh be mi'ty kin' an' good to Fanny?"

"I curtenly will, suh."

"Fanny, will yuh lub Ben an' 'bey him an' sarve him all de
days ob yuh life?"

"I will," modestly yet firmly said the bride.

"Let's pray," said Uncle Harper—and such a prayer.

It was a trifle too long, maybe, for the tinsel trappings of a like
occasion among the gold-knighted dudes and sapphire gartered
immaculates of the "Four Hundred" of New York; but, as the
simple-hearted tide of sweet petition went forth from that

148

humble man of God, black as he was, methinks the angels hard by the throne of mercy and love caught up the words of that prayer, welling up in simple faith from the heart of that dusky old preacher, and in after life brought back full answer to the same in blessed benediction. As the full and hearty "amen" was uttered, the deep response of "amen! amen! amen!" was heard from more than a hundred servants whose ancestry in the jungles of Africa knew naught of God or of matrimony.

"Stand up! Stand up!" said the old preacher, and taking their hands in his, he joined their right hands together, saying:

"Dem what de Lord hab j'ined (joined) together is married. I 'nounces dat Ben and Fanny is man and wife, amen. Salute yer bride, bro'ther Benjamin."

The report, which followed, may not have been so loud as that of a cork from a bottle of old champagne, but it was loud enough to show that Ben had obeyed and it bore witness to the fact that Ben had saluted his bride. Such a salvo as it was. Then came the supper in the kitchen for the bridal party, while ample refreshment was passed around among the servants on the piazzas and in the yard. But not one morsel of cake or drop of homemade Scuppernong wine did the old preacher or bride or groom partake of until "de ole marster and all de white folkses" had been generously served. Then came the feast, attended by such flow of fun and frolic, followed by the dance at the quarter, when Eli's fiddle and Frank's banjo were enthroned in all their high power over these old-fashioned servants, on that old-fashioned plantation, in those old-fashioned days, before the flood of constitutional amendments—when Uncle Harper and the bride and the groom were just as happy as the day was long.

CHAPTER XVII.

Funeral customs.

THE CHECKERED INCIDENTS of the old plantation life, as stored away in the cells of memory, clearly indicate the wisdom of the composers of our well-nigh divine liturgy, when, in one of the collects of the old Book of Common Prayer, human life is referred to under the striking expression of "the changes and chances of this mortal life." Darkness follows light, as does sorrow come so close after joy, that man,

> "That pensioner on the bounties of an hour,
> Vibrates like a pendulum betwixt a smile and a tear."

Soon after the marriage ,which we have just attended came the funeral of little George, a fine lad about twelve years of age, the son of the old ox cart driver, Harry, we last saw at the circus. His death came so suddenly as to cast a pall more than ordinarily deep upon everybody on the plantation, from the old planter down to the present writer, the playmate of the dead boy. Even dear old Buck was sadder far than anyone had ever known him before. The suddenness with which death came to this bright-faced young servant had much to do with the deep sorrow which went over the whole plantation. As in the elemental forms of society it is not infrequently the case that the very strongest hold is had upon the truth, so is it that upon the untutored Indian, the illiterate African, the unexplained and inexplicable mystery of death comes with greatest force. With them it is indeed a fearful reality, with no effort made to explain it away. The death came about in this way, making an impression on my young mind, then a mere boy, which a half century of the stern activities of life has not done away with. This boy often went fishing with me—

carried my bait, gourd, and "toted" the string of fish for me. It was in the autumn when the corn was ready for the early harvest. His father was driving an ox cart heavily laden with corn, and George was sitting on the load, piled up high and kept in place by broad boards on each side. Thus you will see he was mounted high up above the ground. It was about half an hour before sunset when his father, in driving through one of the plantation gates en route home, whipped up his oxen and came through the gate rather hurriedly, passing over a piece of scantling between the two gate posts, occasioning a very severe jar to the load. The boy was thrown from the top of the load of corn with great violence to the ground, and in falling lost his life. He was thrown with his head under him, and it seems the lateral motion of the cart gave a twist or doubling up of his body, which brought the whole weight of his body down on his neck and broke it. In a moment, in the twinkling of an eye, this young African had gone on across the bourn from whence neither Aristotle nor Lord Bacon have returned to bring back any intelligence of the Vast Beyond—illimitable, ever mysterious. Decades have run into each other and a half century has passed since with young, tearful eyes and sympathetic heart, myself a boy, at the supper table that night I listened to my father giving the family a recital of the facts as obtained by him from the poor, heart-broken father. There was more than the moistening of eyes that night as my father told us how Uncle Harry brought the body of his dead child for a mile or more, across the creek, in his own arms, down the avenue to the playground and home of his boy, laying it in the lap of his mother, resting it on her warm, motherly heart. We were told how he was put into a hot bath and all the restoratives known to his profession were used by the plantation physician; but all, all in vain, for his neck was broken, and George was dead. It was the first time in my young life that I stood so squarely confronted by this icy messenger which men call death, and I have never forgotten the deep impression it made upon me. My mother had not yet returned from Uncle Harry's house, where her motherly instinct had carried her, in sympathy for her stricken servant. As she gave us her version of the terrible grief of the mother and the other children we all broke down, while Handy, the dining room servant, hurried out, wailing as he went. Late into the night the voices of those who were keeping watch over the dead could be heard singing their mournful songs, and it was very late before sleep came to any of us, so deeply moved were we by this sad occurrence.

Next morning, Virgil and Jim, the carpenters, were ordered to make a coffin, while Uncle Suwarro gave orders for opening the grave in the little "God's Acre," appropriated to the burial of the servants. In those days, of less hurry than these days, it was regarded as unseemly to bury the dead until the third day—one full day intervening between the death and the burial. On the third day all the dispositions for the burial had been made; the servants from the orchards and the lake, with all the plantation people and some kinspeople from the neighboring plantations, were all there. A very large assemblage it was, so still, so awestricken and, withal, so reverent and so full of sympathy. Ah, how true it is, that one touch of genuine sorrow makes us all akin. The pallbearers were from the boys on the estate, about George's age, and maybe a little older. I well remember I felt as though I would have liked to be one of them —for death is such a leveler of all class and caste distinctions that the grave is a veritable republic. Had not my own mother incited me to deep sympathy with these dusky dwellers in the dark valley and shadow of death? Had I not seen this blessed woman attended by her maid, Eliza, steal quietly out of the sitting room and, as she bade her servant take up her silver waiter, on which was a cross of beautiful white flowers, make her way to the quarter? Ah, a very Evangel she appears to me now—what a very angel of God does this mother appear to her own boy, gray-haired though he may be, as she seems to bear in her gentle hands the two milk-white doves, as it were, of Charity and Religion— going on her way to touch the hearts of these dusky, sorrowing ones, servants

153

though they be, with the more than magic wand of woman's sympathy.

Well, Uncle Harper is there, ready to warn all of the suddenness of death and to comfort, in his simple way, those hearts which were bleeding. He did so from the words, "And Jesus wept." Were not the occasion one of such touching sadness and the presence of death so awe inspiring, one might be tempted to reproduce some features of this sermon in the dialect of the old preacher. But the proprieties of the occasion sternly interdict anything of the kind. Suffice it to say that while the old man's utterances were fully in keeping with the solemnity of the occasion, and more than once his old eyes were the outlets for the welling over of his loving old heart, he at no time ranted or was betrayed into any of the more objectionable forms of emotionalism. In his simple, artless way, he showed that he had a strong, vigorous hold on the keystone of the arch over-spanning eternity, the blessed doctrine of justification by faith in the lowly Nazarene. Then came the singing of that wonderful, soul-anthem, "Jesus Saviour of my soul"—and such voices, such melody! The scene will never be forgotten, through the deep impression made upon my boyish mind at the grave, as the body was being lowered, by all joining the old preacher in singing that favorite plantation funeral hymn:

"Hark, from the tomb a mournful sound,
Mine ears attend a cry;
Ye living men come view the ground
Where you must shortly lie.

154

CHAPTER XVIII.

Autumn.

SINCE the days when there fell from the lips of the old Hebrew prophet the inquiry of God's people, "Is not this the wheat harvest to-day?" there has ever been, with an agricultural people, a peculiar interest in those glorious days of autumn, commonly known as harvest. Poets have sung of the joys which properly belong to it, so blessedly answering the hopes of those who have known the inspiration of the early and the latter rain; while, in sweet communion with nature, they have felt the chemic forces of the sunshine and the dew. The whole plantation was ever glad at this ingathering season. All were very busy in the preparation for winter, storing away most industriously for this less active portion of the year. On yesterday active preparations were going on for the pleasure of the guests of the family, who had now but a few days more before a general breaking up of this band of youth—some to go back to Princeton, some to return to St. Mary's school, and others either to Chapel Hill, the State University or to their homes in Wilmington or New Berne.

The vacation was about to close. Such a vacation of fun and frolic had it been. Uncle Amos had been ordered to make the necessary preparations for a rather exciting hunt for wild hogs in the White Oak Pocoson, which lay to the northeast of the plantation, about five miles away and across the river. This heavily timbered swamp, of many thousands of acres, drained by the white Oak River, was the habitat of much large game, while it was the rendezvous of many hogs which had strayed away from the plantations and, growing wild, had largely multiplied. So the hunt for wild hogs was on and there was a bustling activity, in the preparation of guns, ammunition, and a plentiful supply of provisions for both man and beast. Well, here they go, Uncle Amos in his large mule cart, with a large hamper basket of food for the hunters and grain for the animals, while "Old Bet," as he called the old large-bore plantation gun, was carefully stowed away and his four dogs followed behind. These dogs were half hounds and half bull terriers, showing on more than one occasion their peculiar fitness for this order of sport. The old planter, with his two sons and four other young gentlemen (guests) were well mounted, and as they rode off, each with gun and some with bowie knives, followed by Buck on his mule, they suggested passages in the border life of the "Scotch Raiders,' on their forays for English cattle along the border, in the days long ago. As they passed through the barnyard six mule wagons, horse carts and ox carts were busily employed in hauling up the corn still in the shuck, and already a large pile of the golden grain had been brought in from the fields preparatory for an old-fashioned corn shucking, which we hope to attend.

Corn shucking. Library of Congress; public domain drawing.

Nothing of special importance transpired en route to the hunting grounds, on reaching which the horses were carefully

156

picketed and left in charge of Buck. Uncle Amos called his four dogs to him, patted them lovingly, and in the superstition of his race spit on the head of each one and made a cross mark on the ground, all for luck, then ordered them in for the hunt, himself following as rapidly as the dense undergrowth would allow. On came the party of young hunters, with the old planter in the lead.

What splendid old forest trees are these! What stately cypress and sweet gums! How dense the undergrowth of sour wood and holly, interlaced in some places by the luxuriant growth of the yellow Jessamine, while the bamboos and the cat briars ran here and there and well-nigh everywhere, in their rich luxuriance from the alluvial virgin soil. They make but slow progress, as every now and then some of these city hunters are thrown to the ground, with the foot caught in these vines. Still they persevere. On they go. What sound is that?

"Dat is ole Jube's voice," says the old black Nimrod, as he cries out, "Harky, Harky, Bob! Harky, Saffo! Go to 'im, Pluck."

Presently it was clear that some game was nigh, for by this time all four of the dogs were hurrying on the trail, causing the woods to ring out with their deep-mouthed, musical voices. The hunters pressed on, the old darky gliding along at their head in his mastery of woodcraft, and his old face lit up with all the joy of the chase. Still the cry from the dogs comes back deeper and deeper. Again the old darky calls out:

"Look for 'em, boys! Find 'em, boys!" The pursuit continues. After about a quarter of an hour's pursuit, when the depths of this Pocoson[15] had been reached, Old Amos called out in strong, full voice:

"Ole Marster, dat's no hog! Dat's a b'ar."

---

[15] Pocoson is a swamp or marsh in an upland coastal region. Also, po·co·son, po·co·sen. Origin: 1625–35, Americanism; possibly an arrangement in a southern Eastern Algonquian language.

The well-trained ear of the old hunter had caught the angry snarl of Saffo's voice and unerringly he interpreted it. At this announcement everybody's expression changed. Faces flushed and eyes kindled in high excitement. Uncle Amos was in his glory, for, much as he loved the coon hunt and the pleasure of sneaking along through the grass to kill the bald eagle, watching with keen eye from his eyrie in the top of a tall, dead cypress, his chance of swooping on a lamb or a pig, "de b'ar hunt" was his highest earthly enjoyment. Still the cry of the dogs goes on! The notes become harsher and harsher, deeper and deeper, and the old hunter knew his faithful dogs were pressing their quarry closer and closer. On went the pack, on came the hunters! Splendidly did these young gentlemen bear themselves. Were they not on their mettle? The angry cry of the dogs comes back in such short, snatchy notes as to tell Uncle Amos what to do.

"'Give me de guns," he called out.

Thereupon there was a quick examination of the guns, lest the caps may have fallen off the tubes, for it was before the day of breechloaders.

"Is yuh ready?" he cried out, and with a thrilling ring of his voice he cheered on his dogs. Then he rushed on, but presently stopped, as he heard the yelping cry of one of his dogs. With no effort to conceal his anger, he cried out:

"Dam' dat b'ar; I'll git eben wid 'im yit."

Pressing on, he soon came in sight of Saffo prostrate at the foot of a large white oak, which, partially uprooted, had been bent over by some fierce gale of the equinox at such an angle as enabled the bear to find safety from the dogs some thirty-five or forty feet up the reclining trunk. My sakes! What a pandemonium of fury and noise, as the dogs bayed deep and heavy at the foot of the tree, with their mouths foaming with white saliva and their eyes bloodshot from hot anger. By this time the hunters were all up. Hear the old darky, as in short, quick sentences he indicates the mode of attack.

158

"Dese dogs mustn't git kilt! Ole Marster, you shoot in behind' de fore shoulder! I'll put a lode in his back! Marse John, you an' de odder gentlemens fire into him as he falls! 'Tain't no use shooting him in de head—head harder dan a negur's." As agreed upon, the party of the younger hunters had ranged around the tree at convenient distances for effective fire. The bear, well up the tree, the trunk of which he was hugging with a strong, instinctive grasp of his wild nature—looking around with his big eyes, and mouth wide open, full of dangerous teeth, as the dogs would bay at him in loud and fierce notes, was growling savagely. Presently Uncle Amos and his master, at the signal given, fire as agreed upon. The loads evidently took effect but failed to kill him. As he was falling the old darky fired again and with deadly aim, for as the four dogs seized him he was unable to make any fight. The old man called out, "Dat las' lode, Marster, dun de work, suh. He's done dead."

Thus the old hunter saved his dogs, for in bruin's deadly clutch some of them would have been killed. In an instant his keen-edged knife was passed across the throat of the bear and a large stream of blood flowed freely, which the dogs lapped in their hate of their lifeless enemy. What was to be done in getting the animal to the cart? He was far too heavy for them to drag his body out to the point where the horses had been left. The plan was soon agreed upon. Marse John and Uncle Amos were to return for the mule and cart lines, while the other hunters would take a course with the dogs around to the left, hoping still to find some of the wild hogs. After a time the party returned with the mule and soon the hind legs of the bear were closely tied together and slowly, yet successfully, the mule dragged the bear out of the Pocoson. While waiting for the other members of the party to come up to the rendezvous, several sharp, ringing reports of the guns well around to the left, with the barking of the dogs, assured Uncle Amos, "dat sum game is up." Mounting the mule, he made his way in the direction of the firing. He had not gone very far before he met his old master, who told him that the dogs had run

159

into a herd of wild hogs and, bringing them to bay, the young hunters had fired into the game, killing one and wounding two others. The old hunter's blood was up. He rode on as quickly as he could and pursuing the wounded hogs with the dogs, by well-directed shots dispatched both of them before the dogs were allowed to close in the deadly fight. The kind-hearted old Nimrod succeeded thus in protecting his dogs which he valued very highly. The large boar and two sows were dragged to the cart in the same manner that the bear had been brought out. Soon the cart was well loaded with game and when the sun was about an hour high, the party of hunters rode on ahead, leaving Uncle Amos and Buck to bring up the rear. About nightfall the two servants drove up to the backyard gate, when everybody came out of the mansion to take a look at the bear, while Robert and Washington had been called upon to dress the animal, assisted by two or three other servants.

CHAPTER XIX.

Oyster Roast.

MEANTIME everything was in readiness for an old-fashioned plantation dinner, to be followed by an oyster roast in the kitchen about ten o'clock that night, with dancing coming between the two. As was often the case in those days of unrestrained hospitality, some of the young people from the neighboring estates drove over, and together they enjoyed the oyster roast as those royal entertainments were only seen in the old South. It was yet in the early days of October, and the oysters were not at their best, but had not the month of September, with the letter "r" in it, already passed; and were not oysters good in any month of the year that employed the mystic letter "r" in its spelling? That was the rule immemorial, dating far back in history. We have already been in the old kitchen, Aunty Patty's sanctum sanctorum, ("the most holy [place/thing]") where many offerings were made through this dusky priestess that would satisfy even Epicurus himself. Well, Handy and Buck had piled the logs good and high, and the strong blaze had begun to take serious hold on the wood, when a large iron grate, with railing around some four inches high, was placed on the top of the burning logs. Presently in came two servants with as many oysters as they could well carry piled tip in a large basket. While waiting for the grate to become thoroughly hot, Handy and Eliza had set the table in the dining room with special reference to an oyster supper. To each plate (with it oyster knife and fork) was placed a crash oyster napkin, in which to hold the hot bi-valve. There were no chairs placed at the table, but in the place of the chair sat a large bucket for the shells—for no one ever sits down on an occasion like this to enjoy the oyster at its best. Presently, when everything under the eye of Handy, a most excellent dining room servant, had been put in apple pie order Buck rang the bell, and on Eli stopping the music in the hall in walked, two and two, as merry-hearted a party of young people as town and country could produce. As they move into the dining room what occasions those merry peals of laughter but the enjoyment of some joke of a bad scare or hard fall connected with the hunt for wild hogs that turned out to be a genuine bear hunt? It was quite clear that some of these young gentlemen were making history this morning in their falls, as many an older and distinguished man in politics has done since then—for example, Grover Cleveland. My sakes, what is that Handy and Buck are bringing in in that large wooden tray (well-nigh four feet in length) piled up high and wreathed all around with smoke, as from the cave of Tartarus! Ah, those are the genuine New River oysters roasted a la plantation. The tray is set in the center of the table, equidistant from every point of attack. Hear the ringing musical voice of my elder brother as he calls out:

"Have at them in good style! Let us all set to, as if we were not ashamed of what we are about. Miss Nannie, let me open you some oysters?"

"No, I thank you, I can manage them myself with this thick crash napkin, and besides I do not care to let you see how many I eat."

On the opposite side of the table hear this bit of table talk:

"What is that, Mr. Davis, I hear you say about, 'Women, like moths, are often caught by glare,' when you are caught by a red-hot oyster?"

Here the laugh rang out all along the table while joke after joke went the rounds, as everybody was enjoying the oysters and the bread and butter, with those tempting homemade cucumber pickles. Ah, that hot coffee, strong as *aqua fortis* [16] and toned

---

[16] Latin for "strong water."

down with genuine cream! It was a beverage fit for the Oriental *houris*.[17] But certain it is we do not intend to discuss the supper any further, and right sure are we that it is foreign to our purpose to report how often the tray was replenished or how many bucketsful of shells were borne out; for is not this the table of the writer's father, and true politeness forbids anything more being said on this subject, on the plain principle of the following incident:

When the Honorable Joseph H. Bradley (who afterwards became the Nestor of the Washington City Bar and greatly distinguished himself as counsel for the late unfortunate State's prisoner, Mrs. Surratt)[18] was a young man and a candidate in Montgomery County, Maryland, for the State Senate, in his canvass one day he was invited to dine at the home of one of his friends, who invited him to the sideboard, and there, opening the decanters of brandy and whiskey, deliberately turned his back on his honored guest and walked to the door, leaving him, unmolested by his presence, to help himself. Mr. Bradley used to say that this was the most polite act he had ever witnessed; and, while he had dined with Mr. Clay and Mr. Webster, he had never seen genuine politeness in finer form.

---

[17] Houris are beautiful black-eyed virgins believed by some Muslims to be waiting in heaven for the enjoyment of the faithful, especially men who die as martyrs.

[18] Mary Surratt (1823-1865) was the woman who was convicted of participating in the scheme to assassinate President Abraham Lincoln. She was subsequently hanged.

CHAPTER XX.

Importance of Corn.

THERE was a time in the history of the Roman people, when it was truthfully said in that vast empire that all roads led to Rome. There was a time in the old Southern plantation life that all the roads on the estate led to the corn house. It was, indeed—either in its fullness or emptiness—that the faithful nursing mother of the muscle and brawn was shown to be really and truly the corn house, which was so regularly drawn upon in the general thrift of all forms of domesticated animal life on this large estate. This is illustrated by a common saying among the servants, when the writer was a boy, "Negur make de corn; hog eat de corn and negur eat de hog." Thus, the corn-crop was indeed an indispensable feature, for without it there was no "hog and hominy," no well-kept horses or mules, no crowds of fat, slick, blue-black, little darkies, swinging on the gates, happy as the day was long, singing in their sweet, cheery voices, in melody surpassing the children in the olive groves of Italy, "I Wish I Was an Angel." The importance of this cereal on the estate cannot well be overstated. Hence, every year, some six or seven large fields were given to the production of large crops of this important grain, far more valuable than cotton, sugar, rice, tobacco, or all the other farm products of this plantation. One can now quite understand that large pile of corn, yet in the shuck, so disposed in front of the large corn house and cribs, in semicircular form, as to suggest a fortification—a breastwork against the attacks of hunger in all the oncoming months until the golden harvest came again. How busy all the transportation of the estate must have been to have brought together so many hundreds of barrels of corn from the several fields adjacent! Yet here it is. Some two hundred and fifty feet or more in length must it be, as in form it sweeps around semi-circularly, from one entrance and another to the barn yard, while in height it was some four and a half feet, and in width some fourteen or sixteen feet. How smoothly this immense mass of food has been raked over by cunning hands, and thus made readily susceptible, by measurement, of very exact divisions into two equal parts. Why divide it? Because, in response to a request of the servants, "ole Marster gwine to gib a corn shucking ter-nite, and Buck and Cain dun bin sent round on de mules to gib de impertashuns (invitations) to all de nabers." As Ben thus answers the question, you must observe that his manner indicates no little excitement. This is so because the three great high feasts on the plantation are "Crismus hog killin', and corn shuckin'"— the first an immovable one, while the last two are movable feasts in the African almanac. Pending any one of these notable events in plantation life, everybody is more or less excited and thoroughly occupied. What are Uncle Philip and Uncle Jim doing now? With a tape-line they are making an honest, fair division of that immense corn pile, as nearly equal in bulk and barrels as these well-trained eyes and hands can make it. They have now agreed upon the dividing line, and look how carefully they fasten it down with a long pole laid across the corn pile, held firmly in its place by strong stakes driven firmly into the ground. Old Master is called for and he says the division is just and fair, and that settles it. The estimate is that there are about seven hundred and fifty barrels of corn in that immense pile, which lies there like a big boulder of food that a wave of God's loving providence had swept across the pathway of these sunny-hearted sons of toil. Busy, very busy, are several of the servants in preparing the supper, which always follows. Beef, mutton and pork are in that happy process of plantation cookery known as barbecue, and are in great abundance. Such quantities of bread, wheat and corn, with bushels of sweet potatoes and great baskets of pies and cakes as to require a full staff of these natural born cooks. The carpenters are erecting the simple but substantial tables, and Aunt Daphne is unrolling yard after yard of homemade white cloth to serve as table covers. Well, all the necessary preparations are going on under the eye of the "ole Mistuss," whose judgment with these people is oracular; for this is the fortieth harvest which she has celebrated in her married life. She has learned from the old planter that some two hundred and fifty servants, not counting the women and children, must be fed, and this without stint. As the day grows older and the preparations continue, you observe that the servants are beginning to arrive from the orchards and the lake. Some are busy making their "shucking pegs" of seasoned hickory, while the more fortunate have hunted up the iron or steel ones, which they used last year, and maybe for ten years. The shucking peg is a sharpened spike about five inches in length, fastened at the center to the forefinger by a bit of buckskin on the right hand. With this they dexterously rip open the shuck from the ear of corn held in the left hand, thus saving their finger nails and facilitating the shucking process to a remarkable degree. The dexterity and rapidity with which they strip off the shuck, to one who never witnessed it, are simply incredible. About sunset the assembly bell rings and the servants assemble in front of Ben's house in the barnyard. Here they come, swinging along with that easy motion of body so expressly indicative of good health. No rheumatism here this evening; no stiffness of joints, no aches, no pains. Even old Handy walks along like a boy, while Buck and George are larking around, determined to have all the fun that is possible. Here they come! Here they come! And the cry is still they come!

"My sakes! whay'd all dese negurs com' from anyway! Dey fairly darkens de earth! dey shu'ly duz!" said Uncle Amos as he came up, taking off his hat. "Ole Marster, der's plenty ob 'visions (provisions) for de whole country to eat."

What are those men doing there? They are drawing up two or three of the wagons in position so that from them, as from a stage, "all de white fokeses can jes' hab dere fun at de corn shuckin'," says old Peter, who is attending to this feature of the preparations.

While this is going on, you see some forty or fifty women, boys and girls, some with baskets and others with rakes, getting ready to rake back the shucks from the feet of the men and carry them to those tall rail pens where they will be carefully packed away for the winter feed of the cattle. After half an hour or more has passed, waiting for the latest arrivals of reinforcements, whose deep, rich voices you can hear now coming in several directions from the plantations around, every note of which is full of that peculiar joy so well known to the African ear, and which can come from none other than the old plantation darky's throat,—well, here they all are at last and, before anything else is done, they must all pass in review before the old master, because there are some servants on the adjoining estates that he will not allow to attend pleasure makings of any character on his plantation. They are the disreputable darkies of that portion of the county and regarded as unfit associates for his servants. He takes his position on the steps of Ben's house, and with hats off the procession files by. Presently Uncle Philip announces that Isaac and Arnold are the two chosen captains; whereupon there is a great yell of approbation. These two young men then begin the division of the hands, after a most novel plan to you, dear reader, who have never attended a corn shucking. By this time a dozen or more half-grown boys come forward, their pine torches flaming with bright light, and the scene becomes weird and very animated. Here stand the two captains, and splendid specimens of youthful vigor they are. Here comes Uncle Jim, and as he walks up he takes a knife out of his pocket, saying to the captains:

"Dis is fur de furst choice ob de shuckers," and with that he throws the knife in the air calling out, "Cross or pile?" to which Isaac must make an answer. If he says "cross," and the knife on the ground shows a metal bar on the uppermost side of the handle, Isaac wins on that throw, and vice versa. Then Uncle Jim

168

addresses Arnold on the same conditions he applied to Isaac. The captain who wins the best two out of three or who first guesses twice right has the first choice of hands, and you may be sure they guard their rights almost religiously. Then the choice goes on, each captain choosing his followers until they have gone through the whole number of two hundred and fifty hands or more, each man, as his name is called, ranging himself behind his captain. Then the captains resort to the arbitrament of the cross and pile, as before seen, in the choice of the two halves of the corn pile. The victorious captain, with two or three of his most trusted followers, will then carefully walk over the whole pile of corn, closely inspecting it, so as to hit upon that half which, in his judgment, has the less number of barrels to be shucked, thus making way for victory. After he has decided, he keeps his counsel until they have had a word or two from the old master, in the way of caution against bad temper or any tricks which may serve to irritate or make their adversaries angry. Then, with as much solemnity as any old Greek would employ in consulting the Delphic oracle, the two captains come out to the dividing line of the corn pile, shaking hands in perfect silence, everybody around them as silent as the grave, make a cross on the ground, and spit on it for luck. Then, as if shot from as many Parthian bows, the two captains call their respective followers to them and the corn shucking is on in all its glory. Such noise, such confusion, such bantering, such boasting, until the two captains settled themselves down at the base of the dividing line, marked by the long cypress pole, along which they must shuck through the pile in such a way as not to cause the pole to fall over on either side. The scene, which now ensues, simply beggars description. Dear old Sir Walter Scott, who has delighted the Anglo-Saxon reader of Waverley in his matchless description of the Tournament of Ashby de la Zouche, would fail in its portrayal. The gifted author of Ben Hur succeeding in his chariot race would not attempt it. The author has seen hundreds of men wild with excitement at big fires in large cities—as a young lawyer, when politics ran high in the joint discussion of the old Southern campaigns, he has witnessed how far excitement would sweep men away in wild fury—but these were white men and less emotional than these three hundred Africans ranged around this pile of corn. While the corn shucking is going on and these men are warming up fully to their work, let us look into those wagons over there. The young people from a number of the adjoining estates have come over to enjoy the fun of the corn shucking and the pleasure of the company in the dance, etc., at the great house. It is quite a large company of both sexes you see there mounting up into those wagons, and you may be sure they are having a blessed good time, if laughter and jokes betoken an abandon to fun and frolic. Hear them as they begin to wager, here a pair of kid gloves, there a handsome driving whip or a silver dog whistle, or this and that and the other, on the corn shucking. My sakes! What a chorus of magnificent voices is that we hear as the air is rent with the songs of these corn shuckers. Hear them for a moment as they sing away, the ears of corn flying towards the corn house as thick as snowflakes in a storm, while the shucks are raked away in the opposite direction. Each company seems to have its own leader of songs while all the others will join in the chorus. In all your life did you ever hear such fine voices—some as clear and strong as Kent bugles and others as soft as a German flute. Mark you, the women and the boys and girls are all joining in the chorus. Hear them as the leader, in a clear, strong voice, calls out:

"Massa is in de grate house countin' out his money,
Chorus: Oh, shuck dat corn an' trow't (throwed) in de ba'n, (barn)—
Mistis in de parlor eatin' bred an' honey,
Chorus: Oh, shuck dat corn an' trow't in de barn,
Sheep shell corn by de rattle of his horn,
Chorus: Oh, shuck dat corn an' trow't in de barn,
Send to de mill by de whippoorwill.

170

Chorus: Oh, shuck dat corn an' trow't in de barn."

And then a hundred voices would ring out half a dozen times or more, repeating the chorus until the leader would again call out:

"Ole Dan Tucker he got drunk,
Chorus:
Fell in de fiah (fire) an' kicked up a chunk,
A red-hot coal got in his shoe,
An' oh, Lawd me, how de ashes flew."

And then the full chorus half a dozen times over. The truth is, the scene in all its varied features simply beggars description, and while this is in no wise descriptive of it, it may serve to give the reader some idea of what a full round of melody we would have, when, as was often the case, fully three hundred voices would swell out in the chorus. Meantime the work went on, and the deeper they went into the great pile of corn the higher would rise their excitement, and the deeper and richer their voices in simple-hearted songs. Some of these were descriptive, others simply recitative, in the conduct of which some of the leaders were quite gifted—making up the song as they went along. Frequently it was that plantation incidents, events in the community or the personal peculiarity of some servant would be brought out by the leader in giving a cue to the chorus, which was to follow. No pile of corn, no body of men, could stand up long under such telling work. And yet it went on for two hours or more until the fastest shuckers had gone through the pile and were now about-facing, when the excitement as they neared the close of the race deepened every moment. Stop your talking in the wagon for a moment or two! Listen to those short, quick, nervous cries as they call out, in quivering energy, "Oh, shuck dat corn and trow't in de barn." They show clearly that the race is about to close. Presently as the victorious side wind.; up the race,

171

you would have thought that a cyclone had broken loose, from the way that a cloud of shucks were thrown up in the air, in token of their victory. Two or three of the strongest of the company then caught up the victorious captain on their shoulders and bore him away in triumph to the old planter to be crowned as the victor, amidst such shouts and cries of joy as you, dear reader, have never heard unless at an old-fashioned plantation corn shucking. Corn shucking, not corn husking. White people husk corn, Negroes shuck it—wonderful difference between the two processes is there—quite as much as between the white man playing on his violin and the Negro playing on his fiddle. What a proud Negro captain Isaac is, as his "ole marster" crowns him with a new hat, shakes his hand, drops a five-dollar gold piece in it and tells him to take the other captain by the hand and invite him and everybody else to go up to supper. This he does, and such a crowd and such a supper—plenty and to spare for every man, woman and child there, with Uncle Philip as master of ceremonies, directing Handy, Cain, George and Buck to "wait on dem company negurs fust, after dey dun gib (give) de two captains plenty ob supper an' lots ob good coffee."

In the earlier part of his life the old planter's custom had been to give them plenty of whiskey, but far too many fights and far too much blood were the outcome of the whiskey. He substituted, in the latter days of his life, the best of coffee for whiskey. After everybody had fully enjoyed their well-deserved meal, and, in fact, every feature of the corn shucking, there followed some fine singing of the good old plantation songs, among which were "Old Dog Tray," "Marster's in de Cold, Cold Groun'," "Carry me Back to Ole Verginny," and a half a dozen or more of those old-fashioned songs, when all would go to their homes, not for "de nite," because it's "mos' de broke ob day."

CHAPTER XXI.

Superstitions.

THERE has ever been to the mind of man more or less of mystery about the night. To the illiterate of all races this has always been expressly so. The mind of the plantation darky before the war, was no exception to this role. They illustrated the great truth, operative among all classes and conditions of men, that education holds the only torch whose bright rays serve to dispel the darkness incident to our journey through life.

These people, dwarfed by the ignorance of ancestral environment, were the subjects of many superstitions. They believed fully in all the distorted creations of the supernatural. They held firmly to the sway of witches and recognized the full and often fell power of "conjurers" of their own race. At night they were overmastered very often by their abject terror of ghosts and goblins. The hooting of an owl in the dead hour of the night, or the crowing of a cock near the doorway of their little homes in the daytime, the crackling of the burning brands on their hearthstone, the passage of a squirrel or rabbit along their pathway, the failure to go out of the house by the same door you entered, and many other incidents of their lives, were omens of good or evil, as they had been taught by their ancestry in Africa to interpret them. Up to the date of the events of these pages this race, benumbed by ignorance and fettered by superstition, had not been sufficiently long subjected to the uplifting of association with superior civilization to be fully freed from the sway of these hurtful forces. Fitted or not as they may have been for any other form of manumission, their subsequent history clearly attests the fact that they have not been sufficiently freed from themselves to be clothed, in safety, with the finer forms of American citizenship.

But it is foreign to the object of these pages to present a disputation on the vexed and vexatious race problem in the South. Fortunate, most fortunate, will that man be, who may clear away the difficulties of the situation and speak peace to the American people on this subject. To his memory a grateful people would rear a monument, even more colossal than that already built to symbolize their love and gratitude to that great slave holder, George Washington. Dropping this subject with the comforting assurance that there is a divinity which shapes the ends alike of individuals and nations, let us, dear reader, go and see these plantation people engaged in some of their other pastimes and amusements. While in some sense there was a round of labor from January to December, there were many breaks in it—many seasons and various occasions of what was to these servants fine fun and high frolic. We have seen how much they enjoyed the corn shucking and how fully they could abandon themselves to the circus or horse race; yet we greatly doubt if anything could or did take the place with the old-fashioned darky of the veritable coon hunt. With them, indeed, the possum hunt was a delectation, associated as it ever was with the high feast of "taters an' possum gravy" but after all it was a low form of mere pot hunting. When, however, the darky went out coon hunting his finest forms of energy and cunning were necessarily called out in coping with that "varmint," which so often baffled his woodcraft. The difference between possum and coon hunting was this—the Negro hunted the former for food, while he gloried in a coon hunt for the sport, the excitement in which the fight between his favorite dogs and the coon was exciting and enjoyable, far more so than that of an Englishman contending on a race course, for the Derby Cup. The relations of the dog and the coon ever involved a mystery, which the darky has never been able satisfactorily to solve. As a boy on the old plantation, the writer has often had it thus propounded by his own body servant, Cain:

"Marse Jeems, how doz yuh splain dis: Ole Boss kin whip a possum; a possum kin whip a coon, an' den de coon kin turn rite 'round' an' whip de dog. How yuh splain dat? 'Fore Gawd, dat is mi'ty odd anyhow."

Well, all things are ready now for "de coon hunt." Buck and Cain have provided themselves with plenty of fine light wood for the torches, and Uncle Amos, you see, has his two fine old dogs, Boss and Sappho, following him, as the old man turns away from the grindstone, with the clear light of the torches glinting from the bright blade of his sharp axe, which he carefully hands to his son, young Amos, telling him to be "monstus tickler wid dat axe ennyhow," while the old darky takes up his gun and, whistling to his dogs, moves on to Marse John's office. Here is a party of young gentlemen ready for the hunt, and who are waiting for George and Henry to come on with the axes. So off they started about nine o'clock at night. Everything was favorable—the moon was in its last quarter, the wind was light, and it was just cloudy enough, the old hunter said, "fo' de scent ob varmints to lie rite." The hunting ground was some two miles away along the river swamp, which was heavily set with large cypresses, gums, and white oak timber, with the usual undergrowth of hornbeam and dogwood. The habit of the raccoon is to make his special home in these thick swamps, always near a water course, finding a hollow tree, in which he rears his family in safety; while both male and female will sally out into the neighboring plantation in their destructive forays upon the corn crop while it is yet in its milky or roasting ear condition. They select their den near a stream of water, for the double purpose of being convenient to the fish and mussels found there, of which they are very fond, and for finding a safe retreat in the water when closely pressed by an enemy. The raccoon is not strictly amphibious, but his lungs are so constructed that he can live a long time under water, and thus drown a dog or a wildcat if the two become engaged in deadly clinch. In the laws of instinct how nature seems to take care of all her children, if some of them would only trust her as implicitly as the coon does the water when hotly pressed.

The hunters had been for some half hour or more making their way through this deep forest. The dogs were thrown out on the hunt, right and left, with nothing to break the deep silence save the occasional hoot from an owl out on his foray for food, or the "cheer-up" of the ground squirrel as he scampered away, frightened by the light of the torches, and the suppressed cry of the different forms of larger insect life. Now and then some one of the young hunters, more accustomed to city sidewalks and gas lights than to a night tramp in the forest, would fall over a log or catch his foot in a bamboo briar; when, necessarily obeying the law of gravitation, down he would come—and sometimes spoke a form of English he did not learn in the Sunday-school. The dogs were well trained and the old hunter trusted them implicitly, so on they went, the autumn night wind sighing in the boughs overhead and the silent stars watching in their courses. Presently the deep bark of old Sappho was heard well over on the left. In a moment Uncle Amos cheered on his dogs, calling out:

"Hark to her, Boss; call 'em up, ole gal," and then he said, "Dat's a coon as sure's yuh's born, Marse John; doan' yuh hear de ole gal's voice?"

He pushed on rapidly in the direction of the dogs. By this time both dogs, with fine, rich voices, were waking up the echoes of the lonely woods and showed clearly they were moving the game. The coon, unlike the fox, rarely makes a long lead, but trusts more to the friendly, overhanging trees and the deep water, as a last resort, when hotly pressed. The short, jerky notes of the dogs' voices showed clearly that the trail was a hot one, and Uncle Amos, from his ripe experience, knew full well that they would soon run the game to cover. Presently a very different call from the dogs informed us that the coon had taken to a tree and then the old man broke out with great energy, "Speak to 'im, boys! Gib us de news!

Look to 'im, ole gal." Then he pushed on, followed by the whole party. Soon we reached the banks of the river, where on a tongue of land formed by a lagoon just above us there grew a very large willow oak, at the base of which both dogs were barking in such a furious way as to tell its own story, even if they had not climbed up on the trunk of the tree as far as they could. Uncle Amos spoke up with no little excitement in his voice and manner:

"He's dun up heah, Marse John, suah (sure) as yuh is bawn; dese dogs don't lie, suah. Some negurs lies, but dese dogs nebber; (never) he's up heah an' he got to cum down."

George and Henry were ordered to cut down the large oak, taking care, under the old man's order, to cut the tree so it should fall away from the river. My sakes! How the chips fly, as these two axe men, excited by the prospect of fine sport, throw themselves into the work. While this was going on the old hunter had crossed the lagoon, and with a torch flaming in his hand in the most rapid manner was shining the eyes of the coon. Soon he called out:

"Marse John, yuh make dem negurs, Buck an' Cain, start up a fiah down dere close to de ribber. Dis gwine to take all de lite we kin git."

A few moments later the old man called out in full assurance that the coon was there, well up towards the top of the tree. Meantime, he had built up a large fire on his side of the lagoon, and presently for yards around everything was flooded with light, when he re-crossed and, as he walked away from the tree, measured with his eye the distance he thought the tree would reach on the ground. Then he took Sappho on the other side of the lagoon and asked his young master to please take the other dog far enough away to be out of reach of the falling tree. Just then the great oak, creaking and groaning, as if loath to fall, began at the top to sway and swing. Cried the old man:

"Cut dat lef han' co'ner (corner) quick, boys, and fling her 'way from de ribber, an' look out all han's, fo' de coon is a-cummin."

Just then the tree came down with a great crash; yet before it struck the ground out from the limbs sprang the coon in the direction of the lagoon, but old Boss was a little too quick for him. They closed, they clinched, and such a fight as neither you nor I can describe ensued, while each moment, with great activity, the coon seemed to be getting nearer the water. Just then old Sappho came to old Boss's help. The old darky cried out:

"Keep 'im out'n de watah, boys! Keep 'im out'n de watah, boys! he'll drown dem dogs ef he git 'em in de watah."

After a furious fight for some minutes, just on the brink of the lagoon, the old dog succeeded in getting the coon by the throat and the struggle was soon over.

"He dun got de steel trap grip on 'im now," called out George, and as excitement ran very high among the whole party Uncle Amos allowed the dogs to do him up thoroughly. The coon sold his life dearly, however, for the blood was flowing from the ears and noses of both dogs, as their enemy had set all four of his claws deep down and torn the flesh clear out. While the fight was going on the Negroes were calling in loud tones of deep excitement, "Go fer him, Boss! Hold him, Sappho! Eat him up, ole gal!" After a time, when the fight was over and the victory complete, the old hunter called both of his dogs up to him and examined them closely. When he saw the blood still flowing from the base of old Sappho's ear he took a quid of tobacco out of his mouth and held it there for some little time, thus trying to stay the flow of blood. While he was thus engaged, seeing how deep the cut was from the coon's sharp claws, the old man's temper got the advantage of him and he cussed a blue streak, for the old fellow loved his dogs as he loved his children well-nigh, and maybe you can't blame him so much, as there was no law in old Amos's church against "a Negur's cussin' when dat dam' coon dun tore dat dog's year mos' off."

"Is any ob yuh gemmem (gentlemen) got yo' watch? What time is it, Marster?"

The watches had all been left on the dressing tables at home. The old Negro said, however, "he couldn't see de seben (7) stars nor de pinters, (pointers) but he fairly knowed it was done past midnight and we better be gittin' to'rds (towards) home." So the old man whistled to his dogs—too badly done up for any more coons that night—and the party made their way home, George in the lead, with the coon swung over his shoulder. As they neared the quarter the old darky continued his astronomical observations, as they were now out of the thick forest and he could see the sky. When he found "de seben stars an' de pinter," he said, "it was gwine hard on to'rds one o'clock perzacly." (exactly) And the old man was not very far away from the true time.

Doubtless, kind reader, in this account of the plantation coon hunt, you have been pained, as the writer has been, at the old man's apparent profanity. But, in very truth, when reduced to its last analysis there was no profanity about it. He never employed the name of the Deity. In its use the average plantation servant was as religiously reverent as the strictest Hebrew ever was. Even had he been guilty of the charge, in common charity may we not regard old Amos's weakness as Lawrence Sterne did that of Uncle Toby when he swore; of whose oath Sterne says so beautifully, "The accusing angel, as he flew up to heaven's chancery with the oath, blushed as he gave it in; and the recording angel, as he wrote it down, dropped a tear on the oath and blotted it out forever." Let us hope so, and see what that bright light in Granddaddy Cain's house means at this unusual hour. Marse John said to Uncle Amos:

"I am afraid the old man must be sick; we will go by and see what's the matter."

As they drew near the old man's house they heard a voice; and presently, close by now, they recognized it as the voice of one engaged in prayer. Reverently they paused at the door and listened as this devout patriarch of the plantation, the head of all the Methodist servants on the estate, was pouring his heart out

179

in prayer at the foot of the throne of grace. He was praying with great earnestness, with none other awake in his house than his faithful wife, Aunt Phyllis. Waxing warmer and rising higher in his tide of devotions, the old man invoked the Divine blessing on "Ole Marster, old Mistiss, Marse John, Marse Jeems, Mis' Car'line an' all de white fokeses at the grate house, an' all de negurs on de plantation; an' mak' dem rascals quit stealin' chickens and turkeys of nites." Finally, waxing very warm, he asked, "de Heb'nly Father, pleas', suh, to hab mercy on po' ole Cain, fo' he was tired, mi'ty tired of t'iling (toiling) here below. Pleas', suh, to sen' de angel Gabrul (Gabriel) down an' take 'im home to glory."

Marse John, in a fit of innate badness, could not stand this any longer, and, thinking to put the old darky's spiritual condition and sincerity to the sharpest possible test, rapped loudly on the door.

Rap! rap! rap!

"Who dere?" the old man anxiously inquired, still on his knees.

"The angel of the Lord, come after Cain," in the most sepulchral tone possible, said Marse John.

"Cain; come arter (after) Cain? (Phyllis, put out dat lite, ole 'oman, mi'ty quick.) He ain't been heah, suh, fo' free weeks; he dun gone (throwing himself with great violence well under the bed) he done gone, Marse Angel; ole Marster sent de rascal down to Wilmington wid a lode of bacon an' he dun run away, an' he in de Holly Shelter Pocoson, Marse Angel, rite now.— Lie mi'ty low, Phyllis, an' doan' say not'in' (nothing) nohow," almost in a whisper.

The old man was frightened almost out of his wits. As the mischievous party turned away from the old man's house and were now well out of earshot, old Amos spoke up:

"Marse John, dese heah Mefodis (Methodist) negurs falls from grace monstus quick, doesn't dey? Dase (They've) got none

180

ob de old-fashun' Baptist 'ligen (religion) or de parsavarince (perseverance) of de saints of de Lord."

At his own quarters Marse John found that the other members of the party were already discussing an ample supply of cold ham and beaten biscuit, well-buttered, and such other good things as made up a most comfortable supper for all the party, including the servants, who in their turn ate heartily, all showing clearly that an old-fashioned plantation coon hunt served the double purpose of plenty of fun and whetting the appetite. My sakes! How Buck and all the other servants did eat, while the dogs, Boss and Sappho, enjoyed the scraps. Ah, those blessed old plantation days—we ne'er shall see their like again.

CHAPTER XXII.

Institutions of learning in the Old South. Refinement of the women.

WELL, well, the visit of these charming young people at the old plantation was now over. Comparative quiet now obtained where for the past few weeks that form of sweet pleasure alone known to youth had held joyous sway. They all realized, in the rapid flight of time, how truly Robert Burns had said: (Tam O'Shanter)

"Pleasures are like poppies spread;
We seize the flower; its bloom is shed;
Or, like the snowflake on the river,
A moment white, then gone forever;
Or, like the fitful Borealis race,
That flits ere you can point the place;
Or like the rainbow, evanishing amid the storm.'
No man can tether time or tide,
The time has come and Tarn maun ride." (must go)[19]

Well off to Princeton, to Chapel Hill, to St. Mary's, Raleigh, these young people go; not leaving as they came, however, for

---

[19] Tam O' Shanter, husband of Kate, lingers too long at the market, tippling in the tavern with his friend, Souter (Shoemaker) Johnny. They trade yarns. The landlord laughs with pleasure, and his wife shows herself so gracious toward Tam that, remembering his wife's constant nagging about his drinking habits, he has no inclination to go home, though it is midnight. Besides, the weather outside is stormy and blustery. However, as King Canute, the eleventh century King of England, Norway, and Denmark, demonstrated when he ordered his throne set up at the edge of the sea, even a king cannot control tides or time.

that sly little god, Cupid, had been industriously engaged, and from his bow enwrapped with flowers had sent many a dart with quivering accuracy to the heart. Well, thus has it ever been and thus will it ever be to the end of the chapter of time. Amen. So be it.

The institutions of learning at the South have undergone many changes. Many of them in the late forties and early fifties were far, very far, from lacking very many things to recommend them. When one takes into consideration the fact that institutions of learning in Georgia, South Carolina, and other parts of the South, were of so high a grade that such of her distinguished sons as Alexander Stephens and Benjamin Hill of Georgia, Wade Hampton of South Carolina, the Breckenridges, of Kentucky, and many others whom it were tedious to mention, were outfitted for the distinguished usefulness they achieved, what conclusion do we reach? None other than this—that the wealth of the South (and at that time the nation's wealth was at the South) demanded the best of everything in the markets of the world.

In the world of fashion, Paris, through New Orleans, was tributary to the South. It is said that some of the wealthy people of Louisiana were careful to send regularly their most particular and expensive laundry work to Paris. If it be true that this was the rule in regard to the outfitting of the body, we are quite sure that North Carolina, in common with Virginia and the other Southern States, held within their border institutions of learning—male and female—preparatory schools, colleges and universities, which proved the nursing mothers of both men and women largely influential at home and abroad. We know that this was so in North Carolina for years before the war and, thanks to God, the old State, after a long, dark interval, is coming to her own again, and we believe this is so in the South generally.

The writer is free to admit that the practical working of our system of labor at the South served to keep the extremes of our population far apart. It was a long, long way socially from the front piazza of the planter to the cabin door of either the overseer or the "poor white trash" element.

Practically, before the war we had no yeomanry; and m this condition lay our greatest weakness—compensated, however, by so many advantages under the old regime as more than condoned that weak thread in our social organism. In this cluster of preparatory schools for the university, as well as in the number and high character of her smaller colleges—but more expressly in the university, we have the secret of the State's wealth in great men; while for the perpetuation of that noble race mothers were educated, and well educated—not out of any of the gentle and influential femininities of the sex—as well by the Baptist at Murfreesboro, the Methodist at Greensboro, the Presbyterian at Hillsboro and Charlotte, the Moravians at Salem, as by the Episcopalian at St. Mary's, Raleigh. These institutions, in those blessed good old days, were both the pride of and the bulwark of the State, and served to produce that fine type of character which made citizenship in this State abound in all the finer forms of conservatism. In the markets of the world the State credit was equal to the best in this country; while her merchants were able to buy what they pleased in New York, and on such terms as they might elect. The healthful interblending of the Scotch-Irish blood of the Piedmont and western counties with that of the Cavalier and Huguenot of the more eastern and coastal section, had prepared a race of men whose high courage and devotion in the army of Northern Virginia later on has never been surpassed in the annals of our race. The religious life of the people, happily fostered at her schools, had very much to do with this result.

The writer can speak in none other than a general way of any of these schools except Mr. Bingham's school for boys, then taught in Orange County, some twelve mile a from Hillsboro; of St. Mary's school, Raleigh; and of the university at Chapel Hill.

They were all three exceptionally fine institutions, and naturally enough so, as they enjoyed many marked advantages.

The South at this time was at the very zenith of her prosperity, coming from her great wealth. In those days it was not an unusual condition of affairs that at the same time and from the same family the daughter should be at St. Mary's, the elder brother at Chapel Hill, and the younger boy at Mr. Bingham's school. Thus, in some sense, these three institutions seemed to have gone together, drawing their patronage from the same families between the Potomac and the Rio Grande.

At no institution in this country (not even excepting the famous boy school in Concord, New Hampshire; and we doubt whether we ought to except Rugby, England, in Tom Brown's days), in the last fifteen years before the war, was there annually assembled a finer body of youth than that over which William I. Bingham, the second, presided. It has been a half century since I looked in his fine old face, but I warm up and grow younger when I think of him. What splendid boys this noble old teacher numbered among his pupils. When I shut my eyes and call their names, flushed with young life and its joyous anticipations, I can almost hear the ringing laughter of the brilliant Davy Hall of Warrenton, of that born Chesterfield, William Hunt Hall of Wilmington; of that singularly handsome boy, James B. Hughes of New Berne; and of Henry Cobb of Alabama. Yes, I can see the manly forms of the Merritts; that born linguist of Chatham county, Sam Jackson; and am prepared for all the mischief of Parsley of Wilmington and many others just as attractive, most of whom went with me from this school to Chapel Hill, while many of them have passed over the river just a little way ahead of me, where I trust we may all meet dear "Old Bill," as we then called Mr. Bingham, that nonpareil, that prince of American teachers.

And what shall be said of dear old Chapel Hill, with Governor Swain as president; the Messrs. Phillips and Professor Fetter, Dr. Shipp, the scholarly Hubbard, the amiable Wheat, the faithful

186

Brown, the loving young Battle, a tutor full of rich promise, so faithfully kept in lifelong usefulness to his alma mater and to his State; that miracle of men, in his vast learning, Dr. Mitchell; with that embodiment of high character and consecrated talent, Judge Battle? Old Chapel Hill boy of the early fifties! Shut your eyes and hear the old college bell, while you think tenderly of Walker Meares, Jimmie Wright, John Holmes, Henry Bryan, Baldy Capehart, Alfred Waddell, Rufus Paterson, Tom Settle, Zeb Vance, Jimmie Wilson, Gideon Pillow, Hunter Nicholson, that sweet hearted boy, as handsome as an Apollo, Ivy Foreman Lewis, John Swann Moore, and "Button" Battle; with that youth that never had a fair fight with the devil in his life, but who was born good, Dick Battle; Dick Henderson, Fred Hill, Horace Lacy and Dick Yarboro. Then tell me if you and I did not have royal companions in those days?

Do you wonder that "Ole Bunk," in his tender, watchful guardianship over that band of splendid boys, showed the whole South that he bore the university a far-reaching love which only death itself could reach? His charge, embracing during his long term of office many of the noblest young men of the South, was indeed a grand one; and right nobly did he and the whole faculty perform their loving duties. Their fidelity to high trust was such that in elevating the standard of citizenship in the commonwealth and elsewhere in the South they lessened the duties of those who have succeeded them. Messrs. Battle, Winston and Alderman, as presidents of the university, have all gratefully felt that these educators stimulated them to such alacrity and marked ability as have spread abroad the high fame of this great institution. *Esto perpetual. Esto perpetua longissime.*[20]

---

[20] Roughly, "May it continue for a very long time."

Turning now to another institution, let us attend a commencement of St. Mary's in that golden era of her high prosperity under the elder Smedes, who, faithful unto death, through a long life of such high function as one of the great teachers of the land, has made his name a household word in many houses of the South, even as far away as the Bio Grande. This is Commencement week at St. Mary's, and those carriages filled with youths are just down from the Commencement at Chapel Hill. These young gentlemen, en route home from the university, have stopped over—some to witness the graduation of their sisters and sweethearts, others to have a good time generally. June is here in all her leafy pride and the city of Raleigh is out in full force, with her beautiful daughters and chivalric sons. Wilmington, New Berne, Edenton, Washington, Fayetteville, Charlotte—in fact nearly all of the larger towns and most of the counties of the State are here represented, as well in the young ladies of the school as in the many guests. It is indeed a "red letter day" in the history of St. Mary's. In that large parlor, perhaps the largest, and certainly among the most beautiful in the whole South, what an assemblage of beautiful maidens and handsome young men? What soft, sweet voices these Southern girls have, and what marked proprieties of dress you must observe among them; also how modest their bearing, and the absence of anything like boisterous or bantering demeanor. Not a single touch or taint of a hoyden among them all. Of home refinement and delicacy of the old plantation life, what living and loving epistles are these Southern girls! How proud is their old bishop (Atkinson) of them all—his dear children, most of whom he has confirmed—you may see, as his loving eye lights up with admiration of those three lovely, tidewater girls who glide along over the stage to their places at the piano, harp and guitar! What poetry of motion in the carriage and walk of the ante-bellum Southern girls in those blessed days when the young men did not part their hair in the middle, and when no bicycles had ruined the grace of woman's attractive movement. How broad and full the course of study in this school, the admirable essays, read so modestly and effectively by the young ladies, set forth, as the noble face of Dr. Smedes lights up with pleasure at some singularly fine sentence in her salutatory falling from the lips of that fair graduate from Georgia; or as further on in the exercises the valedictorian moves many of a large audience to tears when with faltering voice she says farewell to dear old St. Mary's forever. Had the present writer a million of dollars a minute for one short half hour (now that in the breaking up of the old plantation life the Southern wealth has gone), five millions should go to the endowment of Chapel Hill, five millions should go to the building of St. Mary's, and five millions should be spent in establishing a large preparatory school, on the same plan as that of the Bingham school in the fifties, giving to every one of the Southern States scholarships in each of these splendid institutions. And yet it may be that these schools, in common with Davidson College, Wake Forest, and all the other schools of our Southland contending with poverty, may in the end demonstrate the fact that the most influential of all endowments is fine Christian character, allied to that broad and deep scholarship which the Southern educators are now bringing to our institutions of learning from the Susquehanna to the western verge of Texas.

When one pauses long enough in these days of hurry and worry to give the subject the thought to which it is entitled, by virtue of its importance in the past to the South's record, no class of her devoted children is more entitled to a grateful recognition than such as have already been mentioned among the educators of the land. To them, among many others, the names of Deems, Horner, Wilson, Graves, John Bingham, Sprunt and Robinson should be added, as those whose lives are perpetuating themselves in the great usefulness of their pupils, their children, and their successors in high office. High office it is. Aristotle and Socrates were great teachers, and yet it was left to the great Nazarene himself to illustrate the fact that he who taught most

189

industriously, with the highest standards always before his eyes, preached most effectively.

The writer could scarcely have said less than he has said in giving anything like an adequate knowledge of the schools to which the Southern boys and girls were sent from their plantation homes, in the good old days before the floods of 1861 and '65. These schools, in the high character of the great teachers of the South, account for the remarkable influence of her people for so many years, actually shaping the policy of the Government for more than three-quarters of a century in affairs of the republic. Their power was only broken under the benumbing influence of the French Revolution, so prolonged as to reach from Paris to Faneuil Hall, Boston, ushering in that form of popular contempt for authority which has swept away the Constitution, having employed "Uncle Tom's Cabin" as its *avant coureur*.[21]

It will not be forgotten that these pictures of Southern plantation life were to be seen in all the Southern States prior to the war, as well in Maryland as in Texas. The writer portrays those in North Carolina, not because they were exceptional, but because he can speak of these more understandingly. The early fifties at the South was an era of high standards. Her prosperity was never greater. The wisdom of her statesmen had been vindicated, in the popular judgment, by the annexation of Texas and the acquisition of California. All over the South, at that time, the public men were of such high character and were possessed of ability so very marked as to show that Calhoun, Clay, Benton, King, Gaston and Beeves had left their impress on that age.

In North Carolina our young men were animated by the example of a singularly strong band of distinguished men. In the Senate of the United States were Messrs. Badger, Mangum and

---

[21] front-runner.

Haywood, succeeded by such men as Bragg, Clingman, and others scarcely less distinguished. In the House of Representatives were McCoy, Donnell, Ashe, Outlaw, Bryan, Craige, and Ruffin, all of whom showed clearly that Mr. Macon's influence over the State had never died out. On the Bench of the Supreme Court were the elder Ruffin, Pearson and Battle; while on the Circuit Court Bench were such pure jurists as Caldwell, Bailey, Person, Shepherd, Settle, Manley, Dick, Saunders and Ellis, all of whom served to maintain the high standard of judicial purity and ability erected by Henderson, Murphey, Daniels and others. Such men as Gales, Holden, Hale, Pulton and others, maintaining the high rank of journalism in the State, with a singularly able and pure body of clergymen presiding over the different churches of the commonwealth, were the influential forces actively at work, in cooperation with the marked purity of home life from Cherokee to Currituck, in investing the State with that power which she showed all through her history, and notably so from 1861 to '65. No wonder that when their old mother's honor was assailed such men as her peerless Vance and her intrepid band of distinguished sons should have rushed to the rescue, followed by one hundred and twenty-five thousand patriots, espousing her fortune for weal or woe from Bethel to Appomattox. This faintly outlined condition of the South in the decade just before the War Between the States was the fine fruitage of her social forces in active play from the old plantation life. She was at the acme of her glory then, and certainly in many respects Christendom has never equaled it. In our subsequent history we can hope for no parallel—in its high-typed golden-hearted manliness; in its gentle, refined and cultured womanhood; in its freedom from the prurient forces of that materialism which measures men, not by what they are so much as by their pecuniary successes altogether. From its fine products we must, indeed, characterize it as a bright era in the history of our civilization. It was about to die. Like the dying dolphin, which puts forth its most beautiful coloring as it gasps out its life on the whitened sands of the seaside, so the old South was never so fair nor so dear to her children as during the last decade of her existence, from 1855 on to the close.

We have glanced at the schools and colleges of the South, and have seen how admirably they served the high purposes for which they had been called into life, by the wealth and culture of the old plantation regime. It must not be forgotten that while the North centered all of her finest energies along the lines of commerce and manufactures, the South, up to the great upheaval, continued an agricultural people (with her great wealth and consequently her strength) on her large landed estates.

CHAPTER XXIII.

Relaxation and amusement.

TO THE Southern people many and varied were the sources of relaxation and amusement. We have indicated some of the home modes of innocent enjoyment on these pages. Few people ever made more of or derived more pure pleasure from the celebration of marriage than did our fathers and mothers, in their old-fashioned, home kept weddings. To the bridal couples of that era there were no limited express railroad trains, taking them with lightning speed out of touch with the loved ones at home. This was the bright reign of home weddings among home people, with the joyousness of home customs and the sunlight of home glorified upon everything. After charming hospitalities at the home of the bride (where the guests, sometimes from a hundred miles or more away, were entertained) the bridegroom's family called all the guests to his home. Then the bridesmaids and groomsmen claimed their privilege of entertaining. Thus was it that one marriage often called for a half dozen or more beautiful parties. Thus was it, also, that one wedding led up to other weddings. One can quite understand the social conditions, where these old-fashioned English customs had obtained from the early settlement of the country. What strong reason had these people for loving their homes, the lares and penates of which had felt no touch or taint of commercialism, and who were strangers to the rude shocks given the divine institution of marriage by the modern appliances of divorce whose fearful driving wheels are centered in the clubhouse. In those better days of the republic, freed largely from cosmopolitan evil, the present writer remembers well the widespread interest and

193

regret over the first notable suit for divorce among the very best people of Virginia and Maryland—how it was discussed and how sharply reprobated. Alas, alas, what changes have come with Worth gowns from Paris and the customs loaned us (in questionable kindness) from Gotham, time is sadly revealing. In those days it was not unusual for parties of young people, properly chaperoned, to spend some weeks of the winter season of gayety in New Orleans, at the old St. Charles and St. Louis hotels. The time ordinarily selected was just before the Lenten season set in, when the charming population of that delightful city, French and Creoles, were at the heyday of enjoyment in the carnival season. The return home was made generally by the Mississippi River, whose floating palaces were singularly attractive. In the summer time the wealth of the South enabled many of its best people, old and young, to repair to Saratoga Springs and elsewhere North. The seaside resort at Cape May was then very popular; nor was old Point Comfort less so, as there had been no development of any kind, good or bad, at Narragansett Pier or Newport. Modern millionarism at that time had not rendered possible such a social evolution as the "Four Hundred" of New York, that sickly product of the distempered conditions of the post-bellum congestion of wealth and morals— of masculine women and effeminate men.

In our portion of the old South there were two occasions of marked interest to plantation people. These were our agricultural fairs and the sessions of our State Legislature. In the summer months there had been an interchange of charming acquaintance among the several sections of the State. Some of the Tidewater people went in their own carriages, in quest of health and pleasure, as far as the charming resorts along the French Broad River, and elsewhere across the mountains in western North Carolina. Others again found all they desired near home at Nag's Head or at Beaufort Harbor. There was no Morehead City in those days. A larger number still either occupied their summer homes, in the healthy sections of Moore and Chatham, or went to the charming resorts in the famous old County of Warren, known in the parlance of that day, as Jones' Springs and Old Shocco Springs. The writer, as a university man, and as a young lawyer, had enjoyed social life at Saratoga and the Greenbrier White Sulphur—had tested the soft crabs and other good things at the height of the season at Old Point Comfort and Cape May—and he is free to say that all this, of its kind, was very fine and enjoyable. At the same time, let these young Southern readers know the fact that nowhere in the world, in the judgment of the writer, did the old plantation element feel itself quite as much at home as at Jones' and Old Shocco Springs. And this is so for these reasons— here the plantation element, from the Albemarle and Pamplico sections of the State, with large wealth and high culture, from weight of numbers and social position, had the controlling influence. These resorts had been frequented by the same families, in many cases, for more than one generation. And then, in those days, the County of Warren, with its great wealth and fine society, was the special habitat of the old-time Southerner. In its palmiest days it is said to have had, on the whole, the finest estates, the best bred horses, the purest breeds of "Alston-Greys" and "Cotton Reds" (game chickens), the largest gardens for both flowers and vegetables, with the most luxuriant mint beds in the whole State. Regarding its higher products, some have affirmed that the men of old Warren were singularly manly and its women exceedingly beautiful. Let it be observed, however, that in these particulars no county or section throughout the whole South had any monopoly. This much the writer runs no risk in saying. Memory, true to her trust, carries him back to one of the most noted of all the seasons at Old Shocco, when the large and fashionable company was at its height. The various sections of the State were represented there, as well by its fine young men as by its beautiful women. It was the evening of the "great ball." Richmond and Petersburg, Virginia, and the larger towns of the State were out in full force. Old Frank Johnson's (Negro) string band furnished the music, and who ever heard better dance

195

music than this? It is said that, as the night 1 wore away, this remarkably gifted darky has often been known to lose consciousness and go to sleep, yet go on calling the figures and never make a mistake. The floor was full of couples in the large, double quadrilles, and "Bright the lamps shone on fair women and brave men."

It so happened that in the same set were two sisters from the neighboring town of Warrenton, and the lovely Miss — from Wilmington, Miss — from Bertie County, perhaps the most beautiful woman North Carolina ever produced, and Miss — from Wilkesboro. These five were the most strikingly beautiful Southern girls the writer has ever seen anywhere. And yet, what am I talking about? What is the difference between the most beautiful rose in the flower garden of Pensacola, Florida, or that same lovely flower found in Richmond, Virginia? One star may differ from another star in beauty, but the characteristic loveliness of the ante-bellum plantation girls was so marked that you could scarcely note the difference between its fine forms, as seen all over North Carolina. You may say the same of the whole South. Two of the above young ladies were types of that form of beauty in the delineation of which dear old Sir Walter Scott seems to have reveled in his description of Brenda in the "Pirate," while the other three represented that order of loveliness of which her fair sister, Minna, has ever been the type. But what is the use of stating that which everybody knows? The beauty of Southern girls has passed long ago into a proverb. Our Northern friends love to come down to Baltimore and witness for themselves the beauty of Southern girls on Charles street, and hear their sweet voices in the mellow, soft accents of the Southern plantation, with no blight or blur of nasal catarrh upon it. The young people of that time delighted in attending the agricultural fairs in Raleigh in those beautiful days of October, where the deep interest and healthful emulation in the plantation products brought many of the most successful planters together. The sweet hospitality of Raleigh, then scarcely a city, together

196

with the Yarboro Hotel, Guyon's, and the City Hotel under that perfection of a host, Captain Lawrence, added largely to the pleasures of the occasion. In those days the fair was not regarded as over until the young people had enjoyed the "Marshall's Ball" at the Yarboro Hotel, a very charming function, under the inspiration of old Frank Johnson's music.

In those days Raleigh was, indeed, a most charming city. How could it be otherwise when such distinguished sons of the old State could then be often seen on the streets as ex-Governor Charles Manly, ex-Governor William A. Graham, ex-Governor Thomas Bragg, Judges Badger, Battle, Ruffin, Saunders and Manly, while the Haywoods, the Bryans, the Johnstons, the Mordecais, the Grimes, the Hines, the Cottons, the Camerons, the Masons, the Devereux and many others kept their ancestral position in society, rather by what they were than as they were rated by the tax collector? Ah, me! *"Tempora mutantur et nos mutumur in Mis,"*[22] said the old pagan. Without employing any vain regrets or indulging any invidious comparisons, it may be pardoned an old man if he says that when such men as the Moores, the Ashes, the Daveses, the Waddells, the Hills, the Grahams, the Collinses, the Davises and many others were active in the State, Citizenship, as worn by them and their brilliant orators, Hawkes, Miller, Joseph Hill and Michael Hoke, was accounted her greatest wealth and proudest distinction, rather than the money of individuals or corporations. It was during this golden era, when these social forces had fully crystallized into their very finest forms that the Legislature was in session. The truly representative men of the State were members of that body, with that peerless gentleman and distinguished lawyer, the Honorable Richard Speight Donnell, as speaker. Raleigh was, perhaps, never so enjoyable as at that time. With her own

---

[22] Roughly, "The times have changed ..."

citizens at their best, in the exercise of that sweet hospitality for which they have been ever so strikingly distinguished, one can say this with perfect impunity. You may be quite sure that such young gentlemen as James Allan Wright of Wilmington, William Saunders, Joseph A. Englehard, and many others like them, were in the full tide of enjoyment of that city, full of charming strangers from various sections of the State. Party after party was given by the Manleys, the Haywoods, the Badgers the Bryans, and others equally distinguished for social position. With its beautiful belles and its striking beaux, the city had never been known quite so gay.

There was one young lady about to make her entree into society and to signalize this important event in her beautiful young life her father and mother gave a very large party. Perhaps it was the most noted event of a very notable winter. The attendance was strikingly large, embracing some of the *creme de la creme* (best of the best) of the State, for these proud parents, on both sides of the house, represented two of the most distinguished families in the whole commonwealth. When the whole house was fully ablaze with light and the old-fashioned wax candles, in untold numbers, were shedding their soft kindly rays (the modern gas or electric light was unknown then) over the large company, surely could Sir Walter Raleigh have walked in with Queen Bess on his arm the "virgin queen" would have recognized no trace of degeneracy in the beautiful women and handsome men. She would have joyously exclaimed to all about her, 'These are the rich products of the Anglo-Saxon civilization, which has girdled the world with life and light and beauty. They are all my children." And well might she have done so, for passingly beautiful was the rare scene. The whole night passed as joyously as that of a belle on her wedding eve. The distinguished debutante was radiantly beautiful, moving about among her delighted guests and receiving the homage of all whom she blessed with her smiles, as does the light of a May Day gladden a bank of roses. Such courtly gentlemen as Judge Badger, the Lord

198

Falkland of the South, and others, gladly paid her homage, and one may be quite sure that we all felt proud of the beautiful Miss — Among the many guests there was one who had grown gray amid similar scenes, but had never married. 'An enforced celibate, he had not borne his lot as gracefully as he might have done, but unfortunately had become somewhat embittered as Cupid from time to time turned his back upon him. When the evening was at its height of enjoyment this gentleman commented, rather in a loud tone of voice, upon the society of Raleigh, remarking in easy earshot of a group of the most charming young people present:

"Miss Charlotte, do you not think the society of Raleigh this winter is strikingly characterized by the extreme juvenility of the beaux?"

This he said not to but at young Wright, who was as handsome as an Apollo, with his face as smooth as a girl's. The young Wilmingtonian turned on him, his fine face flushed with suppressed anger, his lip wreathed in disdain, and said in a clear, ringing voice:

"General, one of the most painful commentaries on man's relation to life is that he is but once a man and twice a child."

Ah, well, these old days have passed away. All that is left of them is for the most part sadly reminiscent. Fortunately, most of the actors in those charming scenes have passed off the stage. Few, only a very few of us are left to chafe under the unhappy changes which a hybrid civilization has brought on. Eating no dirt, spitting no fire, we still hold our colors firmly in our hand, and are yet enabled to cry out:

"Let fate do her worst; there are relics of joy,
Bright dreams of the past, which she cannot destroy."

CHAPTER XXIV.

Christmas on the Plantation

WE have already seen on these pages some of the amusements of the old Southerners. We have witnessed how readily their warm, sunny temperaments expressed themselves, as well in their outdoor sports and wiles as in those around their hospitable hearthstones. Not more surely do climate and soil assert themselves in forest, field, and flower, than in the habits, tastes and employments of those subjected to their sway. The differentiations between the dwellers along our Northern lakes and those of our beautiful Southland are largely the outcome of the difference in climate. After all is said and done, they are far less racial than climatic. Among the many and marked differences between civilized nations, it is a blessed fact that there is one event in their history which, year by year, is asserting a growing influence over all sorts and conditions of men. It need scarcely be said that this is the birth of the Nazarene, the Son of God.

At the South Christmas has ever been known as a season of blessed rejoicing. Among the people of the North, until the past two or three decades, their Thanksgiving, with puritan imprimatur, was a higher feast than that of the Nativity. This grew out of their differences in religious faith and training. Now, however, among all Christian people, there seems to be a fixed determination to make Christmas the one great, precious holiday, not only of the nation, but of the world as well. At the South, in great house and cabin, for generations it has been the season above all others full of mirth and good cheer. Besting from labor, the planter and his servants have ever enjoyed it. From the settlement of Roanoke Island, the Bethlehem story has made its influence felt wherever the Cavaliers have gone. Nor have the Huguenots made it less of a "red letter day" than the blessed doctrine of the Incarnation fully entitled it to. On the old plantation the planters were taught at this season of love to open their hearts and purses to every cry of sorrow and every detail of distress. His Christian mother, coming from old England or the southern part of France, had taught him to remember that Judean midnight sky, across which a star flashed that had never yet been seen on shore or sea. As a child, the old planter had asked his faithful mother to tell him all about that lovely manger, wherein, that December night, the Virgin mother held in her arms that babe, above whose head was an aureole and in whose eyes was the revelation of the brotherhood of man.

On the plantation in the old South no sooner was the harvest well over than slow yet methodical preparation for Christmas was entered upon. The fruits of the earth gathered in, the large stores of animal food well looked after, the planter bent his energy to the fattening of his bullocks and hogs. The butchering season, or the hog killing time, was a joyous event to the servants on the estate. On this plantation it was no child's play to provide the meat rations for so many servants; and there were no vegetarians among them. The truth is, among men the rule seems to be that the lower the form of civilization the more meat consumed. Be this as it may, about November 20 the hogs and bullocks were as fat as they could roll, and "de hog killin'" began. The salt employed in curing the meat in those days was the large grain Turk's Island article that was well pounded or ground by being beaten in long wooden troughs with heavy wooden pestles. This to the young servants was a great frolic, and one could always tell when the neighbors were butchering by the noise of the salt pestles, which could be heard for miles on a clear, cold morning. In order that there should be no loss or waste, and that plenty of time should be allowed for consuming the "chines and the chitterlings," the hogs were not all butchered at once, but with an interval of ten days or two weeks between each killing. In this way the sausage, so deliriously seasoned with pot herbs, the juicy tenderloins, the tempting spareribs, the delicious sweetbreads, and perhaps the most delicate of all, the brains of the animals—in fine, everything coming to the old planter's table at this season of the year—made up a breakfast good enough for a king. The young servants were careful to save every bladder from the several hundred hogs, which they blew up with their own hot breath, introduced through a joint of reed inserted in the neck, and which after being securely tied with bits of cotton string, were hung up over the fireplaces in their cabins. They thus supplied themselves abundantly with Christmas guns, exploding them in place of the modern firecracker, during this high festival.

One can quite understand how rapidly passed the hours during these active preparations for the holidays. The wagons and carts for days beforehand were fully employed in hauling an ample supply of well-seasoned firewood from the new-ground clearings of last winter to the wood pile at the mansion and to every cabin on the plantation. Indeed it was suggestive of cheerful warmth and comfort to see the many cords of oak, hickory, ash and blackjack brought in at this time. The mill wagon, or carry-log, was used to bring in from the turpentine orchards large logs of seasoned pine or light wood, to be sawed up and split for the cheerful fires, so essential to a well-kept Christmas.

The market wagons were now brought into use. Well laden with barrels of lard, turkeys, ducks, geese and other poultry, eggs, butter, roasting pigs (with shuck foot mats, baskets, horse collars and other products of the servants' private industry), they were driven to the market towns of Wilmington and New Berne some eight or ten days before Christmas. These were disposed of by Uncle Suwarro, and the purchases of nuts, candies, fruits and other things, for great house and cabin, were made by this judicious old servant.

At this time the old planter always remembered to send a big turkey and a fine roasting pig to each of several friends in town, who never forgot to send back boxes of oranges, lemons, grapes, figs, runlets and baskets of fine old wine, with some liquids not so light as wine. The merchants never forgot so good a customer as the old planter, especially at Christmastide.

Among other purchases never forgotten was a full supply of bandanna handkerchiefs and Barlow knives, as presents for the servants, while a plentiful supply of strings for Eli's fiddle and the banjo players was always purchased. At this gala season there was from the well-appointed stores of the plantation, a full issue of clothing, including hats and shoes, so that every servant on the estate would be especially well dressed, "fo' Crismus." My sakes! How busy was old Uncle Shadrac in barbecuing five or six whole hogs and halves of young bullocks, taking care to baste them well with a long handled mop that had been dipped into a pan of vinegar, salt and home grown red pepper, so that there should be no lack of highly flavored seasoning. Uncle Amos was very busy in his daily hunts for game—wild turkeys, ducks, squirrels, partridges and pheasants—while the old planter himself saw to it that there should be a saddle or two of fine venison for this occasion. The truth is, nothing seems to have been forgotten by the planter or his good wife. The captains of the vessels trading between our landing and the market towns were ordered to bring up a full supply of selected oysters in the shell, not forgetting salt water fish and fowl, Handy was careful to feed the young gobblers very heavily on broken rice and peanuts, while the several cooks were as busy as they could well be in preparing a bountiful supply of bread (corn and wheat), with cakes, pies and all sorts of good things for the servants' Christmas dinner. Virgil and George had erected long tables in the back yard, while Buck and Cain had gathered quantities of evergreen from the woods, including basketsful of fresh fragrant wintergreen and the delicate mistletoe, with which to dress the pictures and paintings in the great house.

Ah, me! How it delights one to go back in memory and bring back the joyous scenes enacted during the blessed hours of absorbing labor of Christmas preparation. The day before the "high feast" was one of special activity. Everybody was busy. Aunt Daphne and Jane were covering the long tables with white homespun cloth, while the writer's sisters, with needles and thread, were sewing on the borders sprays of cedar, boxwood and wintergreen, so as to make the tables as pretty as possible. The pride of the planter and his family was stirred to make the occasion just as pleasant as possible, alike in the great house and the cabin. The young ladies issued invitations for a cotillion party during the week, while the young gentlemen invited some of the neighbors to join them in the indispensable fox hunt. It often happened that the house was full of company from the neighboring towns, friends of the old planter's children, boys and girls, who had come out to enjoy an old-fashioned plantation country Christmas.

Well, the preparations are all complete. Supper is over and the house is ablaze with light from the many candles, as well as from the cheerful fire. The pictures have all been dressed with evergreen; while large bunches of mistletoe with waxen berries are suspended from the centerpieces of the large halls and parlor. Merry laughter from merry hearts, snatches of songs, the buzz of animated conversation and notes from the piano were all heard, when suddenly a salvo as of artillery startles the merrymakers. What is it? Some twenty-five or thirty of the young servants have come up to give "Ole Marster and Mistiss" a Christmas eve serenade, which they preface with those Christmas guns which startled us a while ago. This loud report is the simultaneous explosion of those hog bladders that were hung up at the butchering season. The young servants put them down on the hard beaten paths around the great house and jump on them with both feet. This is the secret of those loud reports, which broke in on the fun and frolic.

And then when quiet is restored comes the serenade. It is in the form of Christmas carols, which have been taught them by the planter's daughters, and rendered by a quartette of servants,

205

accompanied by flute and violin. The present writer has heard fine singing in St. Thomas' church on Fifth avenue, New York, as well as in the cathedral in New Orleans. Never at any time has he heard more melody evoked than that on these serenades by the fine voices of the servants. To this very hour I can shut my eyes and still hear them, nor have they been displaced by either the roar of artillery at Manassas or the rattle of musketry at Gettysburg. Well, the concert or serenade is over, and Eliza, Handy and Buck have gone out on the veranda with trays of all sorts of refreshments for these thoughtful members of the planter's family, who presently fully refreshed, retire to their own quarters, singing as they go with all the joy in their hearts of the old-time plantation Christmas—perhaps a little bit heightened by a glass or two of good old homemade Scuppernong wine or eggnog.

During the evening orders had been given by the old planter, through Ben, Uncle Jim, Suwarro and Handy, that all the poultry, and every animal on the plantation— including Inez, the pointer, and old Dozy, the jack—should have a bountiful Christmas feed early in the morning. Not that they were not well fed ordinarily. They were. But it was a matter of beautiful sentiment with my father and mother that on the morning of the birthday of the King every form of animal life on the estate should be placed in full sympathy with the Christmas "high feast." The great house was elaborately dressed with evergreen— pictures, halls, stairways and all—when, every disposition for the next morning having been made, the family retired, each to his own department, but not to sleep for an hour or more. All were busy in the opening and arrangement of the different presents for each other and the household servants. It was the sweetest and tenderest hour of the whole year to the family. At this time unselfishness, that virtue which binds man so closely to God, took on its very finest form. Doubtless the angels of God, all aglow with festive joy, were reporting to the recording angel much, very much, of the power of love which is still of heavenly record, though the actors for the most part have long since passed away. While these ministrations of family friendliness were going on, often after midnight, the silence was ever and anon broken by some young darky firing off one of his Christmas guns, for the joy of this warm-hearted, emotional race was wholly unrestrained at this blessed season. What a difference in its observance here by these Christianized Africans and their kinspeople on the banks of the Congo and Loango in the far away "dark continent."

My sakes! What a fusillade that is. Bang! Bang! Bang! "Hurrah for Christmas!" No more sleep. The day is breaking and Christmas has come. Listen to those merry voices down at the quarter! It would seem that everybody is awake, from Granddaddy Cain, the old patriarch of the plantation, down to the youngest little ebon-faced darky. All up and very fully awake, one would say, if the ringing laughter and joyous greetings pass for anything. Nor is this Christmas joy confined to the servants at the quarter. The old mansion is full of the opening up of various forms of festivity. Hear the ringing shouts of "Merry Christmas, father!" "Merry Christmas, mother!" "Christmas gift, ole Marster; Christmas gift, Ole Mistiss," coming from Handy, Buck, Eliza and all the other house servants. The custom of the family was, as each one came out into the breakfast room to bring with them their presents for the other members of the household, placing them on a side table, beautifully dressed with flowers and evergreen, prepared for that purpose. After family prayers these packages, properly bestowed, were all opened. In many cases, what display of perfect knowledge of each other's exact wants! How beautiful some of them are, while no one is forgotten—not even Buck, George or Cain—for, at this season especially, the old planter's home is a republic of love.

Why is it that of all the family the ole Mistiss, the dear, blessed mother, the devoted wife, receives more presents than any other? The answer is easy. Her many presents are the tokens

207

of that tribute exacted by her boundless love for us all. Ah, the far-reaching tenderness of motherhood!

What nice little package is that you see the old planter opening there? He opens one wrapper, and yet another, and another, and another, until at last he comes to a box, as of fine jewelry. While he is opening his treasure observe that beautiful young lady from New Berne, as she watches him very closely. At last he opens the box and takes out the most cunning contrivance. What is it? It is of the finest flesh-colored silk. The dear old gentleman holds it up between his thumb and forefinger so that everybody can see it, still no one seems to know what it is. At last one of the young gentlemen (who seems to be the master of more than one of the fair donors' secrets) calls out:

"Why, don't you all see it's a nose protector—something to protect the nose from the cold when out fox hunting of a bitter, frosty morning? Pray, sir, put it on please."

"Put it on; put it on," was heard all around the table.

Sure enough the dear old gentleman put it on his rather large, Napoleonic nose, and how nicely it fitted and how everybody enjoyed the joke, as he wore it with the delicately wrought holes for nostrils and the cunning little pink and white tassel suspended from the tip end of the nose. What a roar of laughter and how the dear old planter enjoyed the fun, as he turned and thanked Miss Nannie D. — for just what he wanted, telling her he would be sure to wear it; and wear it he did on more than one bleak winter morning when fox hunting. Well, the presents are all opened—and such an array. A dog whistle of silver, a beautiful riding whip, kid gloves, a prayer book, stationery, a beautiful silk dress, something from each one for all, not forgetting presents for the servants of the household.

Handy rings the breakfast bell and we all sit down, amid peals of laughter, to such a breakfast as the present writer will not attempt to describe; simply saying that his mouth waters, even at this late day, when he thinks of the broiled oysters, venison steak and beaten biscuit, with hot rice waffles and such coffee.

Breakfast over, the assembly bell rings. By the side of a table on the back veranda the old planter and his dear wife take their places, while all the servants file past them, each receiving some present —a bandanna handkerchief, a Barlow knife, a doll baby or a package of tobacco; and to each of the foremen an envelope with a crisp bank note in it, everyone calling out in passing by, "Merry Cris'mus! Merry Cris'mus!" and right merry it was. After church in the morning, to which all went who were so disposed, the wish of the old master bringing about a large attendance, the family enjoyed a luncheon at one o'clock. At two o'clock the assembly bell rang and the servants assembled in the back yard for dinner. Before they began their dinner the prizes in money were given for the first, second and third best crops in the turpentine orchards that year.

It would have done you good, dear reader, to have seen Ben, Uncle Philip, Cicero and Robert serving as special waiters while dispensing this excellent dinner of barbecued meats with plenty of potatoes, rice, corn and wheat bread, followed by pies and cakes, with coffee in abundance. Ah, you ought to have seen the festive joy of these overgrown children, as nicely dressed, amid peals of laughter and the frequent explosion of their Christmas guns by the younger ones they fully satisfied their appetites. I will not humble myself by undertaking, and then failing, to describe some features of this plantation Christmas dinner. I certainly do wish, kind reader, you could have witnessed the company manners of the ebon beaux and dusky belles, as they sought to make headway in each other's good graces. How you would have enjoyed witnessing the saucy tossing of her head, bedecked with red ribbon, as Kate, the young mistress's maid, replied to Ben's inquiry, wishing her a merry Christmas. He said:

"Mis' Kate, how duz yer corporashun seem to sergashiate (?) on dis yer 'cashun?"(occasion)

To which suggestive question Kate made reply:

"I am, suh, no wusser (worse) dan I was, but I feels much mo' comfortabler sense dinnah; yuh must hab s'posed dat whole

209

barbecue wuz prepared for yuh. I jes' wish all ole Marster's negurs wuz as 'dustrious (industrious) in de co'nfield (cornfield) as yuh is at dis table."

Wonderfully given to big words at all times, it was on just such occasions as this that Ben would abandon himself to what he called "long tailed bookionary 'spresions." (expressions) Whatever may have been the immediate effect upon each other of such passages at arms as the above, it was true that more than one wedding on the plantation followed close after the Christmas holidays. After these bows and conges and the full enjoyment of the dinner, each one made his respects to the old master. Then, in family groups, they retired to their own homes. As they passed along the well-worn pathway, every few minutes off would go one of those Christmas guns, whereupon in strong, hilarious voice one of the many revelers would call out, "Hurrah for Christmas; Christmas comes but once a year; if I gits drunk you needn't keer." At night they would have their dance and gladly entertain their friends from the neighboring estates, and so this blessed holiday was observed among these people.

Nearly all of these older servants have gone where "de good darkies go," and it is feared that the generation which has come on since these golden hours are strangers to many forms of innocent enjoyment which obtained in those days. The beautiful Christmas dinner, which engaged the family around the hospitable board of the old home was a very masterpiece of housewifery in all its departments. It is rather strange, and somewhat humiliating, that those things which give us the most pleasure in some cases, baffle our powers of description. Among them is an old-fashioned plantation dinner and, I may add, the description of a beautiful bride; for (let it be said respectfully in her presence) the two, as far as I am concerned, baffle all powers of description. Many improvements have come in the last quarter of the nineteenth century—among which are electric lights, telephones and automobile carriages (not bicycles or multiplied divorces)—but the culinary art, as did eloquence and rare statesmanship, reached its perfection in the days of Calhoun, Clay and Webster. There are other features of this festive week which claim attention, and they furnish the writer with a welcome excuse for hurrying over that dinner, the perfection of which would be marred by any attempt on my part at description. We hurry over the description, but there was no hurry in the discussion of the meal itself. After dinner with its black coffee and cigars, came whist, music and a few quadrilles, winding up with the Virginia reel. Thus ended a typical Southern Christmas Day, but the holiday and its festivities extended to the New Year.

CHAPTER XXV.

A Fox Hunt, A Cotillion, and more on the pleasures of Christmas.

OF the accomplishments of the boys raised on the Southern plantation, there is one the acquisition of which he has no clearly defined recollection of. In his nursery days he has a vague remembrance of a pony, of which he acquired a thorough mastery before he put on pants. He knows when and where he learned to swim and to shoot a gun, but from his very cradledom he was made familiar with his horse. Hence it was that, until the resources of the South were broken in the late Confederate struggle for Independence, the cavalry, which followed the standards of Hampton, Stuart, Ashby and Forrest have rarely if ever been equaled in the annals of war. When the Southern boy added to his knowledge of horses that of familiar acquaintance with dogs, which comes only from early and close association, one is quite prepared to find his characteristic manliness. Of the two, the dog and horse, it is still a mooted question that in point of high instinct stands next to man. Loving both of them, the writer will not undertake to settle this question. He will make no invidious discrimination between his friends. Where the two are closely thrown together, as they are in the fox chase, man has ever found ample field for his love of both. This close association of the three most noble forms of animal life—man, horse and dog—accounts largely for that peculiar fascination which the fox chase has ever had for the youth of the South. Far more fascinating is it than a stag or deer hunt. Incomparably superior is it to the bear hunt. Stale and flat are both duck and partridge hunting in comparison with it. This is so because in none of these is there to be found that close comradeship which is inseparable from the rider, his horse and his dog, and which belongs only to the old-fashioned fox chase. Baseball, golf, yachting, lawn tennis, and all of these more conventional, artificial modes of enjoyment, in point of excitement—that tension of nerve coming out of a sense of danger, that high form of thrilling pleasure of the full cry of hounds in close and hot pursuit, that full sympathy between the hunter, his horse and his dog, are not to be compared with this old-fashioned plantation sport.

We are now to speak of one of these. It was at dawn of day, the morning after Christmas, when the silvery notes of our neighbor's (Mr. Frank Thompson) horn were heard floating over field and forest, telling in their friendly way that the invitation to the hunt had been received and accepted. In an orchestra the liquid notes of the cornet are singularly sweet. To those swayed by music, the violin, the flute, the piano and the guitar are very attractive; but the writer has heard nothing so moving, so inspiring, as the mellow sound of the hunter's horn, that harbinger of field sport unequaled. The call is answered. Presently in comes Mr. Thompson, accompanied by two or three neighbors, while the barking of his pack challenges the old planter's dogs, who answer back from their closely kept kennel, telling significantly that they are ready for a trial of speed—for a day of splendid sport. Hot coffee, with cold meats, bread and butter, make up the hunters quickly dispatched breakfast, for the day is fine. The horses are held at the front gate by Cicero, George, Buck, and Cain, the dogs are whining impatiently to be let out of the kennel and the cigars and pocket flasks have been attended to by Handy, when the command is given for the start. Quickly they mount their impatient horses, the gate is opened, out rushes as fine a pack of foxhounds as ever followed game, and the party of ten or twelve hunters ride away as merrily as if they were going to a feast.

Time fails us in describing each hunter and his fine mount. We will, however, take the time to pay our respects to that princely Southern gentleman—our neighbor and friend—Mr. Frank Thompson, whose sons are still actively engaged in keeping up the old line in the dear old county of Onslow. The father had a marked advantage over his boys, in that while, perhaps, he knew less of books than they did, his outdoor education had been more closely attended to and he had developed into one of the most ardent sportsmen in Eastern Carolina. On this occasion he looked every inch the typical Southern foxhunter.

Then about thirty-five years of age, in weight somewhere about one hundred and forty pounds, straight as a Parthian arrow, in height about five feet ten inches, with deep auburn hair brushed back behind his ears under a jaunty hunting cap, mounted on a thoroughbred bay mare (in politics a Henry Clay Whig), he was for all the world the man you would have selected for a hard rider, a close friend, and a hard worker in a political campaign—the wrong man to make angry unless somebody was to be badly hurt. Yes, yes, what a splendid party of true Southerners this was, riding along briskly to the Christmas foxhunt, in those blessed days before the flood. They have all gone over into the borderland and joined the great majority save one. Sad is the thought that their places have not been—cannot be—filled, for the social forces that produced them died out with the old South. Well, the hunting ground has been reached. It lay west of the lake, well out in the turpentine orchard, and above the headwaters of Chapel Run. The dogs, eager for the chase, are circling well out to the right and left, searching anxiously for the trail. The hunters are chatting away merrily about crops, politics, and the weather, as they ride along full of energy and that peculiar élan known only to the genuine foxhunter. Presently the deep notes of old Staver's voice are heard calling for help to carry the trail, which that industrious old dog has found. The old planter cries out, "Hark to him! Hark, Nimrod! Hark, Fashion!" On they ride. The scent is strong, so strong that Mr. Thompson calls out, "By George, it's a bitch fox! Hark, Juno! Hark, boys! Hark, away!"

Rapidly we ride on, for the dogs have caught the trail and have gone. Now the whole pack is calling out in fine chorus. Every hunter has gathered up the reins and straightened up in his saddle, not unlike a squadron of cavalry about to enter a deadly charge. The horses show from the quick way in which they are bounding along, that they are in full sympathy with the increasing excitement of the riders.

The old planter leading his boys, all splendidly mounted, rides like a young man. Ah, what a splendid figure was his that day! The writer has ridden after Ashby, has seen Stuart when mad

216

amid the high carnival of war, but he has never seen any man on horseback more thoroughly the master of his mount than was this old planter when fired by the wild excitement of the chase. The cry of the pack increases in volume, as the trail grows hotter and hotter, while on they go, pressing after old Reynard, who has not yet risen from her cover in the dense thicket which we are now approaching. We have reached it. It was one of those jungles or thickets full of bamboo and catbriers, with dense undergrowth. No horseman can enter it. The dogs go in. Not very far do they go when the sharp, harsh, angry cry of Fashion is heard. All understand it, dogs and hunters alike. The fox is up and has broken away from cover. Did you ever hear such a cry in your life? Hear the deep notes of Rover, joining with the sharper notes of Nimrod and the sharp, raspy staccato of Fashion, while twenty others join in the chorus. The fox, hot pressed, must come out of that dense cover. They are making it too hot for her. Out she comes and, trusting to her speed, stretches away for dear life across the pine ridge clear of undergrowth—about two hundred yards in the lead of the pack. As she clears the thicket, Neighbor Thompson gets a view of her. Hear him, as with his manly voice he calls out, "Hark! Hark! Hark away, boys! Hark, old Juno!" Out they come—the whole pack—and on they go, running still by scent, Juno and Fashion abreast, with all the others following close after! And now comes the sport. Horses, riders, dogs, all full of it. They ride like mad, the old planter and Mr. Thompson leading, followed closely by the others at a breakneck gait, and all yelling as if the furies had broken loose. The fox had too much start and reached another bayou just in advance of the pack, but she had no time to throw away. Into this dense thicket she plunges and rapidly makes her way through it, then leaves it for a hundred yards or more, circles around, and on her back track enters it on the other side, in her crafty cunning hoping thus to elude the dogs, which were moving more slowly through the sharp-set catbriers, the thorns of which are cutting their noses and ears so that the blood flows freely. Some time elapsed before the dogs succeeded in forcing her from cover. After a time old Staver gives out one of those sharp, angry barks which the hunter understands to mean quick work. She has broken cover again, and this time the dogs are close on her; not yet quite in sight, for no fox, red or gray, could ever stand long before Fashion running by sight. So fleet is the good old dog (the most beautiful thoroughbred English fox hound the writer ever saw) that she always reminded one more of the splendid movement of a greyhound in her magnificent sweep of splendid speed than an ordinary dog of the hound breed. On they go! The dogs are running rapidly now, indicated by the short, angry, half-suppressed cry as if they had not time to bark. What rapid riding! What shouting! How much the horses seem to enjoy it as, pulling away on the bit, they rush on. Hard run, the fox just makes the cover again. She has no time to talk to Bre'er Rabbit in her hurry. On come the fastest of the dogs and into the cover they plunge. Here they show their high instinct by circling around singly; and thus, presently, they force the fox out for the last time. Once more she makes a bold, strong lead across the open woods. The old planter and Mr. Thompson are sitting on their horses at the edge of the swamp just as the game breaks from cover, and at the top of their voices they call out, "Here, here! Hark, Fashion! Hark, Juno!" On come the faithful dogs, and as they stretch away across the ridge the two leaders get a glimpse of the fox, and with an angry, sharp scream of a bark they dash on. Reynard's days, her minutes, are now numbered. The hunters ride on. They see that her danger signals are flying, for her tail is down and her tongue is out of her mouth. They press on. Just then, as they are letting their horses out at full speed, they see the fox chase in all its wild excitement, in all its finest form, dogs, fox and horses all running in full view. Then they hear the two dogs, as they utter a half growl and a half bark, and in a moment more the chase is over, for the leading dog overruns the fox, which, in doubling back, is caught by the next dog and in a trice thrown to the ground and fastened by the throat. Mr. Thompson, our guest, in a moment dismounts and with a quick movement of his pocketknife severs the tail from the body. Then with a blast or two upon his beautifully polished hunting horn he calls for the lagging dogs and hunters, inserts the brush in the band of his cap, and, as the victor of the hunt, proceeds to tie the dead animal to his saddlebow. But the hunters are not all up. Waiting some time, several of the party go back to see what has befallen the absentee, one of the young gentlemen from the city. Returning on the line of the last lead from the swamp, they find him some half a mile or more away. He is half reclining at the base of a pine tree, pretty badly hurt. His horse had fallen by putting one of his forefeet in a stump hole while running, when both horse and rider had gone down with no little violence, hurting neither of them seriously and luckily breaking no bones, though giving the rider a severe shaking up. The horse was soon caught, with some help the young hunter mounted, and the whole party started for home. As they jog along, the hunters all agree in regarding this as a very fine chase.

Certainly the bold, strong leads, which the fox had made from one cover to another, embracing in one a lead more than a mile, had put both dogs and horses on their mettle. Undoubtedly it was a most exciting scene in the second fine dash, when the game broke away with a strong lead— after her cunning trick in doubling and running fallen logs in the tangled, thick cover— with all the dogs in a huddle as they came out and took up the hot running trail. It was a scene worthy of Rosa Bonheur, when close after the pack, the hunters let their horses out to a fine speed, cheering on the dogs with exciting voices. Yes, the battlefield has its excitements wholly indescribable, with its roar of artillery, its blaze and rattle of musketry and its bursting and ricocheting shells. Yes, that is so; yet the fox chase of the olden times had a wonderful fascination over those who were trained to its finest forms in the old plantation days—when the high-strung Southerner stood so related to his sunny life as to know what was meant by the saying, "Time was made for slaves."

The whole party dined with the old planter that day, when there was some fine conversation, as Mr. Thompson exploited his dog, Juno, and the old planter came back at him by telling how Fashion had led the whole pack. Ah, those blessed old days! We ne'er shall see their like again; but their memory is very precious to some of us, who have outlived most of our friends, and along whose pathways the dark shadows of the Appomattox have fallen.

The party breaks up, after making an engagement to try their hand at a deer hunt when the dogs and horses shall have rested up. The next day one could have told from the quick way in which the servants were moving about that some important event was on hand. What was it? It was the large party that was to come off that evening. Handy and Buck were busy in waxing the floors of the broad halls where the young people were to enjoy the dancing. The young ladies and young gentlemen were busy in freshening up the decorations—some replacing with fresh evergreen anything that might have withered, others bringing in from the greenhouse beautiful flowers and potted plants. Our young friend who had been unhorsed in the fox chase was out again, still lame but able to assist the young ladies in trimming the candelabra with ivy leaves and other evergreens, and in doing such other things as were necessary. At the junction of the two broad halls a platform had been placed for Eli and the other musicians, so that with the same music four quadrilles could go on at once in the four sections of the broad halls. Time fails for a full description of the elaborate preparations. It is not necessary. We can trust the dear old planter's wife and daughters to have everything just right. Parties were no new things to them. The day wore on. The afternoon was far spent. Towards nightfall the guests began to arrive from a distance. From Clinton, Kenansville, Kinston, Trenton, as well as from New Berne and Wilmington, the guests came. How graciously were they received! What kind inquiries were made of the old fathers and mothers at home. What a marked absence of anything like the chilling, mechanical stiffness of the more modern, artificial manners of certain other sections! What an absence of stiffness in bearing and manner, both upon the part of the guests and those whom they were gladdening by their visit. How easily everything seems to go on. How readily Eliza and Kate (dressed up in their "best bib and tucker," with becoming turbans wound around their heads, and their snowy white aprons) showed the young ladies upstairs. How bright were the faces of Buck and Handy as they escorted the young gentlemen to Marse John's quarters! Where in the round world are all these charming young people to sleep to-night? Never you mind about that. Wait and see. Our early supper was soon over, allowing plenty of time for elaborate toilets before the full opening of the festivities. Now the servants are busy in lighting a hundred or more wax or spermaceti candles (the old planter allows no lamps in his house), when presently the whole house is radiant with light. The guests from the neighboring plantations are beginning to arrive. The parlors are already well filling up with beautiful young ladies, exquisitely dressed, with no suggestion of décolleté or anything like immodesty in their elaborate and rich toilets. Diamonds and pearls, which had been in the families from Revolutionary days, throwback glinting rays of light from the beautiful persons of these lovely young girls. What fair scene for a painter it was! I cannot describe it, but I well remember it. How full of kind courtesy and gentle dignity in their bearing were the young men, who in after years rode with Hampton and Ashby or who) followed where Pettigrew led at historic Gettysburg!

Presently the sweet notes of the violin are heard. The) buzz of brisk, breezy conversation and the rippling laughter of joyous young maidens gives place to the dance. It is no wonder. The young people of the old South, true to their blood and training, were always ready for this innocent amusement. How handsomely dressed are these young gentlemen as they file out, each one with a lovely girl on his arm, for they have heard the call to the dance? Yes, they have all heard the long-drawn notes on

Eli's violin, and his fine strong voice as he calls, "Pardners fo' de fus' cotillion." From the large number of young people present, to furnish the four sets of eight pairs each was not a difficult task. In a short time, apparently, all were ready. Just then someone called out, "Not yet, we are waiting for our host and hostess to open the dance." After some slight delay out came the old planter, with his wife leaning on his arm, and took their places among the young people in the dance. It was a joyous sight in those happy old times to see the two generations moving together in time with the music as they threaded their way through the mazes of the dance. With no disposition to berate the present generation because they have it not, but rather to speak of the exact conditions of society in those days, let us note well the graceful carriage of the young ladies now on the floor of this old plantation home. How do their easy, graceful motions, with scarcely an effort marking the time, seem so exactly to accord with the rich garments so nicely fitted to their beautiful, well-rounded figures. These lovely Southern girls seem to have mastered the pleasing secret of the poetry of motion. Observe for one moment that black-eyed, rich brunette, as with her partner she sweeps along so gracefully the whole length of the quadrille and with her fine face lit up with the excitement of the occasion she flings back a laughing banter to conventionality and says, in her fine motion, "I learned what I know of the finest forms of grace of person from my horseback rides, and not on a bicycle; I love the dance, because in it there is no harm, for my mother spoke truly when she said we commit forty times more sin with our tongues than we do with our toes." Yes, it is true, that as these girl were taught to row a boat and ride a horse they well-nigh mastered the secrets of feminine grace in their carriage and their fine bearing in the dance. Just how far technique in music has destroyed melody, how far the bicycle has robbed the young ladies of this age of graceful form and motion, I know not, but you may judge how graceful these young ladies were if you will only look on at this dance, full of the festivity of Christmastime in the early fifties of the last century. One cannot leave these older people, engaged with their whist and conversation over there, and stand here for ten minutes watching these young people "chasing the glowing hours with flying feet," without saying most heartily that Keats was right when, in his "Endymion,"[23] he said, "A thing of beauty is a joy forever."

On goes the dance—quadrille after quadrille—until long after midnight, with here and there a waltz introduced, and occasionally a schottische or a mazurka, and here and there time allowed for the lancers. The announcement of supper brought in some young people, who were far more seriously engaged in those slow, deliberate promenades on the long piazza which told so unmistakably that Cupid was not dead, but that the mischievous little god was very much alive and very busy this evening. Supper over, the dancing is resumed, until at last, amid the wee sma' hours of the morning, the order rings out from Eli's well-known voice "Git yo' pardners fo' de ole Verginny reel." What a stir! What commotion! Presently it would seem as if everybody was in that dance, the reel reaching the whole length of the hall. Let us count them. There are over thirty couples in this reel. Ah, the glorious old Virginia reel; what memories it evokes, what shadows it proclaims! There are many forms of fine amusement among the young people in the South. The young men love the fox chase and the young ladies delight in their horseback rides, as well or perhaps even better than they do Sir Walter Scott's works or Macaulay's fine essays. The Virginia reel, however, stirs them as nothing else can. It is the last of the dance for this time, and such a dance! It has always been a mooted

---

[23] "Endymion," a poem by John Keats, was first published in 1818. Beginning with the line "A thing of beauty is a joy forever," "Endymion" is written in rhyming couplets in iambic pentameter (also known as heroic couplets). Keats built the poem on the Greek myth of Endymion, the shepherd beloved by the moon goddess Selene.

point whether the reel was made for the Southerner or the young people of the South made for the reel. There is that in the rapidity of its action—a fine field for the natural grace of this warm-hearted, pleasure-loving people—the inspiration of the music in the old pieces of "Grey Eagle" or "Fire on the Mountain" combining to account for the popularity of this dance, which neither wars nor revolutions can destroy. Of its kind—and it is a glorious kind—there is nothing of all the European dances nor of those colder, more mechanical, icy figures of the conventional "four hundred" in chilly Gotham which can match it. Some of those fine, manly forms we see to-night were seen later in the serried ranks following Stuart, Hoke, Gordon and Pettigrew as they followed Stonewall Jackson, who in turn was led by the matchless Lee, but, fine as they were, here to-night they appear to even greater advantage than when they periled their lives and, in so periling them, felt of the edge of battle. Yes, when the Cavalier and Huguenot blood met, as it did here to-night, they showed beyond peradventure that "knighthood was still in flower" in those dear old days of the South.

The hospitality of the neighboring estates was so marked and his own capacity to entertain his friends was so great that by crowding his male guests, and with free use of pallets, the planter's company was comfortably entertained.

The Christmas festivities were very far from being confined to the white people, as the servants had their full share of it in their own way. This was clearly shown by the notes of music, snatches of songs and the peculiar noise, all their own, of "double shuffle," "the break down," "chi'kin in de bred tray" and the graceful "pigeon wing," followed by their genuine "cake walk." Thus did these two races dwell together—the weaker (in daily contact with the older, stronger civilization) steadily emerging from the shadows of paganism. In view of what is now transpiring among this same race in Illinois and Georgia, to the mind of the writer it would have been far wiser not to have made the attempt to hurry Almighty God in His slower, wiser purposes with this race. They were not fitted for the ballot when it was thrust upon them. They were being gradually and healthfully prepared for it, under the slower processes of the relation, which they sustained to the white people under the Constitution prior to the emancipation proclamation. For it is true, absolutely true, that colonization societies were actively at work all over the fair Southland, gradually and healthfully setting on their feet those who a few generations ago were amid the jungles of far off Africa.

CHAPTER XXVI.
CONCLUSION.

Like the last of the Mohicans, the old planter and his race are dead. —Author's ideas on why there are twenty-nine black men imprisoned in the South, out of every ten thousand, in the North the proportion is sixty-nine out of every ten thousand.

IN closing up a volume like this, one finds so many features of great value have been omitted from the picture that, after all, nothing better than a mere sketch has been presented. The writer puts down his pen, saddened by the thought that only a mere outline of the true conditions has been given. On the other hand, if he has portrayed the old South faithfully others will take up the work, so that the grandchildren of the men who were with General Lee at Cold Harbor in 1864, or with General Grant in Appomattox (in other volumes from other pens) will have a more detailed account of those halcyon days in which the South developed such strength as she showed in 1861 and '65.

The reader will perceive that the writer, in justifying his own people—in vindicating his own mother and father, has entered into no argument with Mrs. Stowe. He has simply answered her book, not by dialectics but by statistics—not by getting into a bad humor but by stern facts. Did time and space allow, gladly would the writer go on, enlarging upon those social features of Southern life in the ante-bellum civilization which so strikingly characterized the old South in Georgia, Kentucky, Maryland and Texas—in fine, all over this lovely portion of the country. He would gladly lead you into the boyhood homes of the Hamptons in South Carolina, the Hills in Georgia, the Breckenridges and Crittendens in Kentucky, the Yanceys and Currys in Alabama, where you would at once recognize the identity, except in shaded details, of those forces in all her fair borders which made the old South what she was, the idol of her own people and, from many points of view, the admiration of the world.

He sincerely hopes that none of his readers will regard this volume as either partial or provincial, because he lays the scene of his recitals in one chamber of the old Southern plantation home (and that the North Carolina room) while he knows, and you know that from the Susquehanna to the Rio Grande the same roof-tree, with umbrageous branches, covered the same people, the product of the same institutional forces, speaking in varied dialect the same language, listening to the same song birds, strengthened by the same traditions, gladdened by the same folk-lore, while in childhood we drank in the same lullabies from mothers trained to high duty, and were inspired by fathers incited to the prowess and manliness of their ancestral standards with such hallowed and hallowing community of suffering as, please God, has enabled the whole South to suffer and grow strong.

In having in the pages of this volume, looked upon one picture; pardon the writer if, with a sad heart, he now asks you to look upon another portraiture—that of the present condition of a manumitted and enfranchised race—the same race, only under very changed conditions. We submit, in all candor, that neither in uplift of character nor any qualification for happiness or usefulness has the Negro, as a race, been improved by the change. The writer may be pardoned if he introduces some current testimony from the Philadelphia Record, as startling as it is suggestive:

"In an address recently delivered by Professor Wilcox of Cornell University, before the American Science Social Association at Saratoga, he showed crime is very largely on the increase among the Negro population of the country. But the most startling fact shown was that the Negroes in the Northern States are worse by far than the Negroes in the Southern States.

While there are twenty-nine black men imprisoned in the South, out of every ten thousand, in the North the proportion is sixty-nine out of every ten thousand. This disparity can hardly be explained as a matter of latitude. In the North there are larger opportunities of education, but possibly a lesser opportunity of profitable employment and a more uncompromising prejudice of race. Talk as we may of the difficulties the nation has been called upon to contend with in dealing with the mixed races in the East and West Indies, the problem is not more complex than our immediate home problem; and our hundred years of experience has not furnished a solution."

Twenty-nine black men imprisoned in the South to sixty-nine black men in the North, out of every ten thousand of Negro population of the two sections, is truly startling. "In the North there are larger opportunities of education," Bays the Record, notwithstanding which there are more than double the number of criminals compared with the South. This particular feature merits very careful consideration and investigation. Do the "larger opportunities of education" tend to development of the criminal instinct to a greater degree in the Negro than in the white race?

But the further statement, which may be taken rather as the explanation of this difference, is entitled to the attention of the colored people themselves. It is a fact that the Southern whites are the only real friends the Negroes have, ever have had, or ever will have, but which these same misguided people have stubbornly refused to believe. The Record admits, notwithstanding the "larger opportunities of education," even to the extent of mixed schools in most of the Northern States which may have contributed largely to the demoralization of the Negro—"there is possibly a lesser opportunity of profitable employment and a more uncompromising prejudice of race." This is both an honest and, we believe, a truthful statement. And this condition, mark you, kind reader, exists where there are only hundreds of Negroes to thousands in the South. All of which

229

suggests the inquiry, Has not the South been entitled to, and is it not deserving to-day of more of sympathy than of the censure it has received at the hands of the Northern people for her efforts to solve the problem of self-preservation, while at the same time she treats the Negro humanely? Glad, indeed, are we to state that from frequent expressions of late, similar to that quoted above from the Record, all true patriots are warranted in thinking that the Northern people and press are awakening to the awful ordeal through which the South has passed and through which it is still endeavoring to pass, and in consequence are more disposed to do justice to all concerned. Let us hope a more enlightened and a more just sentiment is developing in all sections of the country, amid the closing hours of the nineteenth century.

Had we time, dear reader, before you and I say "Hail and Farewell!" gladly would we go back to the old home and enjoy ourselves once more at the dear old planter's hospitable dinner table. Well, let us go, anyhow, for we shall not enjoy such royal company again for a long time, if ever. Handy is ringing the dinner bell, and with the old planter in walk a few of his close friends. As they sit down at the table let us look at them somewhat closely and observe the fine products of the old plantation social forces. Whose is that benevolent face on the right hand of the planter? That is the Honorable William Horn Battle, now of the Circuit Court Bench of the State and later on of the Supreme Court Bench, at a time when the people honored themselves in the selection of such gentlemen as the elder Thomas Ruffin and Richard M. Pearson as judges, not for a term of years, but for life or good behavior. Judge Battle is spending the interval between Jones and Onslow courts with my father. In point of high character and the fine forms of great usefulness, the State has had no son more highly respected or beloved; nor has she produced one whose children can, with greater cause, rise up and call his memory blessed. The gentleman on the opposite side of the table is the Honorable William Shepperd Ashe, M.C., the closest personal friend my father ever had. For years he

230

represented his district in Congress, having fully entrenched himself in the confidence and high esteem of the State in the Legislature. Later in life and notably so during the war, he devoted himself with marked ability and high success to the railroad transportation of the South, in which he greatly distinguished himself in that he rendered invaluable services to the people in this most important department. Of distinguished Colonial and Revolutionary ancestry, which he honored by a long line of useful service, his very strongest feature of character was his supreme loyalty to his friends, who, in his tender judgment, could do no wrong; even if the correlation of this be true of him, that his enemy could do no right. In many ways his son, Captain Samuel A. Ashe, of Raleigh, North Carolina, reminds his friends very strikingly of his noble father. The other gentleman, is the Honorable Thomas Ruffin, a member of the North Carolina Bar, but more strikingly distinguished as a member of Congress and still later on as a colonel of cavalry in the army of Northern Virginia; where, at the head of his regiment, he laid down his life in defense of the principles of government for which he had battled so nobly on the floors of Congress. All over the fair South, dear reader, might you have looked upon just such pictures of high character and marked ability. But the writer has drawn this one, in order that the character of the products of the old plantation life might stand out in bold relief before you .There are many portions of the old South which I would gladly visit with you, but the time is close at hand when you and I must part. I would gladly go with you to Edgecombe and Orange counties; to those two dear old Colonial towns, Wilmington and New Berne; to the Piedmont section of the State, at Morganton and elsewhere, there; to the Valley of the French Broad in Buncombe and other picturesque counties; in fine, all over the State; assured that you would readily account for the population from the country they inhabit, in part, but mainly from the religious home life they led, with the uplift given them, each man "dwelling under his own vine and fig-tree;" with the fine social forces of the old plantation life, under which they were taught "to eat no dirt, spit no fire, ride a horse and speak the truth." In whatever direction you might look or go, dear reader, whether amid the savannahs of" the Gulf states or the broad rolling prairies of Texas, amid the blue-grass country of Kentucky or along the now classic streams of Maryland and Virginia—all over the Southland this picture would have been reproduced, with only some slight differences in light and shade.

Like the last of the Mohicans, the old planter and his race are dead.

> "The breezy call of incense-breathing morn,
> The swallow twittering from the straw-built shed,
> The cock's shrill clarion or the echoing horn,
> No more shall rouse them from their lowly bed.
> For them no more the blazing hearth shall burn,
> No busy housewife ply her evening care,
> No children run to lisp their sire's return,
> Or climb his knee, the envied kiss to share."

Dead and yet to memory dear. Yes! Yes! They will live as long as Memory is true to her trust and Virtue stands crowned by a grateful posterity. This book "The Old Plantation," may be read by few or many. It matters not. But the heart in the old life—the social charm in the old life—the loving confidence between the two races in the old life—the high integrity in politics and devotion to the Constitution of the old life —the beautiful form of womanhood with the striking type of manhood in the old life—all growing out of their religious homes, faithfully guarded, under the conservative forces of the old life—these—these shall never fade away. Old planter! Hail and farewell! But not forever, for we shall meet again on the bright plains of the Great Beyond, where no "civil equalities" exist, but where justice, holding the scales, is administered by a God of Love. Hail and farewell! *Zoe mou sas agapoe!* "By my life I love you."

232

EPILOGUE.

IT may be true, aye; it *is* true that Southern nationality is a dream of the past. A gulf, beyond which we could not pass, yawned between us and the realization of our hopes; and though bright flowers bloomed upon its brink and wafted us sweet perfume, we could not cross to gather them. The Southern Cross no longer gleams out amid the wild light of battle; the sword of the vanquished is sheathed, and the land is gloomy with the harmless sepulchers of our martyred dead. But when years and years shall have passed away; when the last of the present generation sleeps with their fathers and new forms throng the old familiar places; when faction shall have hushed and justice holds the scales, then as bright as day and as free from blemish and stain will stand forth in bright relief upon the scroll of historic fame the record of the old plantation South, dearer to the hearts of her children now in the hour of sorrow that when on the march to victory she won the admiration of the world. Pilgrims from other lands shall tread with reverent step above the spot where molders the dust of our loved and lost; while those who are to follow us will cherish as household gods the names of those who, carving their way through the fiery path of war, have written their names where they can never die. The old plantation home life is dead, and the principles for which so many laid down their lives may not be recognized until their names have grown feeble on the tongue of friendship and been dropped in dead silence from the ear of the world. But it is struggling back from the hollow bosom that once bled for it, and will ascend the heights of government at the hands of a reunited and strengthened people, with no sectional triumph upon it. And when the faithful historian shall descend into the vaults of the dead past in quest of traditions of liberty, and in honest search for the facts of history, he will then discover to whom the world is indebted for the perpetuation of the republic. He will find that in the old home life of the South, where such men as Macon and Gaston of North Carolina taught posterity to revere the Constitution and to love liberty, the very finest forms of loyalty and patriotism were installed.

The End

Made in the USA
Columbia, SC
25 May 2020